Voices of
Woodhall Spa

A Century of Memories

by
Marjorie Sargeant

Published by Woodhall Spa Cottage Museum
Iddesleigh Road, Woodhall Spa, Lincolnshire.

Copyright 2003: Marjorie Sargeant.

ISBN: 0-9546443 01

Typeset, printed and bound by
F. W. Cupit (Printers) Ltd., The Ropewalk, 23 Louth Road, Horncastle, Lincs., LN9 5ED.
Telephone: 01507 522339, Fax: 01507 525438, www.cupits.com

Cover picture: 1910. Ladies stroll up the Broadway.

Preface

My aim in this collection of memories was to record social history of the Twentieth century, based in Woodhall Spa.

Occasionally, "younger elderly" (bright young middle-aged) have been included because of knowledge of a certain topic. One or two residents were disinclined to contribute and I may have missed interesting input from others of whom I was unaware. I apologise to anyone who feels left out.

Facts have been checked and I hope are correct but events are remembered differently. Similarly there is some repetition because noteworthy occasions are commented upon by many contributors. I have tried to select a variety of remarks.

I feel privileged to have been entrusted with these personal recollections and touched by the patience shown during long afternoons talking with me. Thank you all.

I would like to acknowledge the support given by many, especially the Trustees of Woodhall Spa Cottage Museum who have, bravely, undertaken to publish the project.

I am most grateful to David Radford, Chairman of the Cottage Museum, for the provision of recorded material which he, so wisely, collected in the past.

I would like to thank Ann Houlton for her interest and enthusiastic rooting out of photographs. Permission to reproduce photographs has been obtained wherever possible.

Background information was obtained from:
"The Horncastle News"
"The Book of Horncastle and Woodhall Spa" by David N. Robinson
"Half a Century of St. Hugh's School" by the late H. D. Martineau
"The Kinema in the Woods" by Edward Mayor
and Log books of St. Andrew's School, Woodhall Spa.

Readers who find these reminiscences interesting will, perhaps, be inspired to note their impressions of current events, thereby becoming voices of the Twenty-first Century.

A postcard of 1908.

1911. "I don't think we shall go to the Coronation tea . . ." is written on the postcard.

Introduction

The story of the beginning of Woodhall Spa is well known. In the nineteenth century, far from city lights in rural Lincolnshire, several parishes converged near the small settlement of Woodhall. Here a dreamer named John Parkinson conceived the idea of digging for coal but the enterprise was unsuccessful and eventually abandoned. However, water which had hampered the efforts of the miners, bubbled to the surface and rumours began that this brackish liquid had mysterious qualities, beneficial to man and beast.

The Lord of the Manor, Thomas Hotchkin, hearing these tales, tried the water for himself and found that it did, indeed, ease his gout. Now the principle that water containing certain minerals had curative powers was popular, both in this country and on the continent, so, in the 1830s, Mr. Hotchkin built a small bath house and, by the end of the decade, a "neat and unostentatious hotel." The water was analysed and found to contain quantities of what were considered beneficial chemicals – Woodhall Spa was born! The hotel, at first referred to as the New Hotel and the Spa Hotel, was named after the new queen, 'The Victoria Hotel' and was enlarged to become an elegant and imposing building.

Over the following years the Spa gradually developed, a pace which quickened with the coming of the railway between Lincoln and Boston in 1848 and more particularly with the opening of a branch line from Horncastle to Kirkstead in 1855. Hotels, boarding houses and houses were built and entrepreneurs introduced businesses to supply the wants of a clientele, which grew steadily in terms of numbers, wealth and social class. Many ordinary householders seized the opportunity to make extra money by taking in paying guests or providing apartments for visitors in the Season.

The local newspaper 'The Horncastle News and South Lindsey Advertiser' was first published in September 1885. At first there was little mention of Woodhall Spa, although occasionally there was an item of news under the heading 'Woodhall.' Later the paper began to publish Visitor Lists of those staying at all the hotels and boarding houses during the Season of summer months. The grandest and most illustrious visitors stayed at The Victoria. Their chauffeurs, valets or maids could be accommodated at reduced rates.

The fame of this spa spread. According to the newspaper, the number of people travelling here by train increased from less than 16,000 in 1886 to over 47,000 in 1889. The Horncastle News of 12th July 1890, reported 'The Season at this fashionable place seems now to have fairly set in. Week by week lists of visitors are increasing in length. It is gratifying that persons of the right class are arriving.'

Woodhall Spa had arrived.

Before the Golf Course was constructed.

Sitting in September sunshine, 1907.

CHAPTER I

Leslie Chapman Esq.

Mr. Chapman, who lives in Witham Road, Woodhall Spa, is frequently seen about the village and is recognised by many. This is not surprising as he has lived here all his life.

Few people seeing him, straight and trim, without either spectacles or hearing aid, would correctly guess his age. He truly looks years younger than he is. For Leslie was born in 1909, when Edward VII was King, Herbert Asquith Prime Minister and Lloyd George, Chancellor of the Exchequer. It was in that year that Blériot made the first air crossing of the English Channel and Leslie was a boy of three when the Titanic sank.

Far from such newsworthy events, this village was, nevertheless, well known as a fashionable spa. Thousands of visitors, including titled aristocracy, arrived during the Season, from April to October and, as well as undergoing medicinal rigours, enjoyed strolling in the Pine Woods and listening to the Spa Band, which played daily in the Bandstand near the Pump Room.

The story of Leslie's earliest days is dramatic and touching. One fine afternoon a local couple were walking in the countryside, where Woodland Drive is now. It was wild and lonely, the only sound being occasional bursts of birdsong and the swish of the breeze in the grasses. Suddenly they stopped, astonished, for they could hear a baby crying quite near to them. That baby, just two weeks old, was Leslie. Now Mr. and Mrs. Chapman, who lived in Mill Lane, had recently had a baby boy who, sadly, had not survived. When Leslie was found it seemed like a miracle, they took him and brought him up as their own, although Leslie always knew and accepted that he was adopted.

One of his earliest memories is of being in a pushchair, with his mother, at the end of Mill Lane, waiting for his father to come with his week's wages so that they could buy their 'provisions'. Leslie's father was a delivery man for the brewery at that time attached to the Railway Hotel near the River Witham. In 1912 his wage was twelve shillings and sixpence a week (62½p).

Leslie has a delightful photograph of himself, aged three, holding a metal bucket and spade and wearing a Breton-style sunhat above a large lace collar – very different from play clothes of today!

He attended the National School when he was five. Mr. Fairburn was Headmaster. At some stage he contracted Rheumatic Fever and, as happened in those days, he missed a whole year of schooling.

The Mill House at the end of Mill Lane was the home of the Rose family. They were bakers and, as well as serving local people in their shop, they also catered for events such as the annual Revesby Show. There were three sons, one of whom owned a Model T Ford – the first car Leslie remembers in the village. The two Misses Rose, Florence and Emily, had a toyshop, crammed with toys and cards, next to where the Co-op is now.

By 1915, when Leslie was six, Woodhall Spa boasted three bakehouses, three grocers and three butchers and the population had grown to 1,656. Its growth and prosperity as a spa had been made possible largely because of the railway. It was an exciting venture to board the train, when it arrived from Horncastle and be taken to Boston, where that carriage was hooked on to the back of the Grimsby to Kings Cross train.

There have been many new buildings in Woodhall since Leslie was a boy and changes in old ones. In an extreme case a complete bungalow was moved! It belonged to Dr. C. J. Williams of the Spa Baths, who used it as 'a sort of laboratory'. It was next to the Golf Hotel where there is now a house. Lady Guggisberg, who was a friend of Lady Weigall, at Petwood, had the bungalow moved next to Jubilee Park, on the left of the entrance drive. Then she had

Leslie Chapman as a boy.   Leslie Chapman in 1942.   Leslie with his 90th birthday cake, 1999.

Woodhall Spa C. of E. School, 1921. Back row: T. Clarke, G. Semper, N. Bell, J. Bass, N. Inman, L. Chapman and C. Rose. Front row: Miss Capindale (teacher), G. Hardy, E. Middleton, J. Bycroft, J. Roberts, S. Gault, O. Hopps, A. Ward.

another built next to it and Mr. Jack Fletcher, gardener at St. Hugh's School and later, Chairman of the Town Council, moved in. He was to look after her place when she was away! Shops have altered many times and some buildings have disappeared. At the crossroads corner, where the small piece of ground with flower tubs is now, there was once 'Chapman London and Manchester Stores. High Class Draper, Grocer, Tea and Provision Merchant'. As Leslie points out, older people still call it 'Chapman's Corner'. After Chapman's the premises became Kirkby's Cash Store.

St. Hugh's School opened in 1925. Leslie himself, aged 16, had left school and started his apprenticeship 2 years before this but he recalls the interest of local people in this new venture.

The Baths and old Pump Room look 'a dreadful mess' now and it is difficult to imagine past elegance but in olden times there were changes. In the early 1930s a Mr. Lewis came to be in charge and he put up wire fencing which restricted access round the Baths. A town meeting was held, protesting about this, at which Mr. Lewis appeared. He was angrily thrown out but Sir Archibald Weigall said he ought to be there to answer questions, so he was dragged in again!

When Leslie was a young boy, life centred around the village, which the family rarely left. In his early days at home there was no mains water. The Woodhall Spa Water Company had been formed in 1909 and water was supplied from a reservoir on Kirkby Lane (where there is now the Nature Reserve). However, the pipes did not extend to every part of the village, including Mill Lane, so residents there had pumps to draw water. Later, when the piped supply was extended, there was a tap at the gate of Leslie's home, which was shared with next-door neighbours.

At first also, there was no electricity. When it did become available one light and one electric point were provided, free, in each room. Before that the house was softly lit by hissing gaslight downstairs. To see in the dark upstairs, it was necessary to carry a candle, taking care that it was well away from clothing and curtains and not in a draught, which would blow it out.

The Chapman family, like many others, kept chickens and a pig, which was killed for Christmas. The carcass was hung up to store and Leslie remembers carving meat off it for his mother to use in cooking and baking pork pies.

It was a big event, once a year, when the family travelled to Navenby (between Lincoln and Grantham) to visit Leslie's grandmother. His father borrowed a horse and trap for the journey. They went by the most direct route which crossed Blankney Park, the estate owned by Lord Londesborough – there was no golf course at Blankney then.

Church on Sunday was a feature of life in the early years of this century. In Woodhall Spa there was St. Andrew's Church of England at the crossroads, St. Peter's Church of England on the Broadway, the Roman Catholic church of Our Lady of the Sacred Heart and St. Peter, two Wesleyan Methodist Chapels and a Primitive Methodist Chapel. The latter, on Mill Lane, is now boarded up but bears the date 1834 and the exhortation 'Hear and Your Soul shall Live,' carved above its doors. There was also a Presbyterian Church on Mill Lane and Leslie attended the Sunday school of this on Sunday mornings, the Witham Road Wesleyan Sunday school in the afternoon and went to the Primitive Church service with his parents in the evening! He laughingly comments that, after all this Nonconformist upbringing, he was married in a Church of England!

When Leslie was still a boy the Chapmans moved over the river where his father worked on a farm. During World War I a Zeppelin dropped a bomb which landed near the old Stixwould Ferry. It was Harvest time and men had been working on the land from dawn to dusk. When Leslie's father arrived for work the morning after, the farmer, Mr. Atkinson, who was a special constable, said he hadn't wakened him to help in the night because he realised how tired he was. At the end of the war, in 1918, Leslie remembers hanging up a Union

Minstrel Group, 1923. A concert given by scholars and friends of Witham Road Methodist Chapel on the stage of the Pavilion (now the Kinema). Trained by Mrs. L. Richardson. M. Rose, L. Chapman, C. Blake, V. Gazeley, C. Rose.

Photo by J. Wield, Cottage Museum Collection.

The bandstand by the Pump Room, 1890s.

Photo D. N. Robinson.

Jack outside their cottage. In future years when he was working at Hundleby's, near the crossroads, the shop was always closed briefly, so that he and his staff could go to the War Memorial at 11 o'clock on the 11th November, to remember the end of World War I and local men who had died.

Entertainment, in the pre-Kinema days of Leslie's childhood was, largely, home-made. There were, of course, grand concerts and entertainments during the Season but, for people who lived here, social life revolved around village societies and churches. Leslie was friendly with Harold Howsam, a keen Methodist at Witham Road Wesleyan Chapel and they always took part in the Whit Monday tour of the village, helping to decorate the wagon beforehand. The organ and choir went on the four-wheeled dray and it set off from the chapel. The first stop was at Hopp's shop on Station Road for ice creams and, after going round the village, the tour returned to Witham Road for tea and races which were held in a field on Mill Lane. Leslie also remembers concerts in the Pavilion (later the Kinema) in which local children took part. One performance, innocently enjoyed at the time, would certainly be unacceptable today. The children were 'little niggers' with blackened faces and they were dressed as minstrels, holding cardboard banjos made for them by a teacher.

A dreadful event in 1920 was the fire at the Victoria Hotel. The burning down of this, the Spa's largest and grandest hotel was a disaster after which Woodhall Spa never recovered its former glory. Leslie recalls that the only part left was the Public Bar, which was where there are now two semi-detached houses, facing the Baths.

In 1922 when Sir Archibald and Lady Weigall returned to their home, Petwood, after his two year Governorship of South Australia, Leslie was in the crowd of villagers and children waving and cheering at the roadside, as their carriage drove past. He says that Lady Weigall was thrilled by the attention, smiling excitedly and seemed quite touched by this welcome. 'To us they were like royalty' he comments.

When he was fourteen Leslie was apprenticed to Hundleby, the grocer. There were two shops, one in Station Road (now a Farm Shop) and one over the river, in Martin Dales, which was where he began work. This was in 1922. The shop was open from 8am to 7pm (8am to 9pm on Saturdays) and his wage was 8 shillings a week. He received this when the shop closed on Saturday evening along with a measured out paper cone of sweets. Over the four years of his apprenticeship, his wages increased by four shillings, annually, until he reached the grand sum of £1 0s 0d a week. At this time, before Kirkstead Bridge was constructed, the River Witham was crossed by a toll bridge. It cost 1 penny a day or 4 pence for a horse and trap and 5 pence for a horse and dray. Nostalgically, Leslie remembers those days when the grocer knew his customers and their tastes and there were weekly orders and deliveries – so very different from today's 'Do it yourself' supermarkets. A smiling face and a good memory were essential, as well as a comprehensive knowledge of stock. He also remembers the hard work of those days without pre-packaging. He tells his story:- 'I always wanted to be a grocer, from the days when Mr. Hundleby collected Mother's order each week and it was delivered, next day, by horse and dray. I remember, as a small boy, going into the Dales shop and looking at all the brightly labelled jars and the big cheese and staring into the tins of biscuits. Sometimes there was an elderly gentleman checking the books. He was Mr. Lunn from Horncastle, the Lunn of 'Lunn and Dodson Grocers' and the 'Co.' of 'Hundleby & Co.' He was the father of the three Misses Lunn, who ran the Girls High School in Hartington House and of the founder of 'Lunn's Tours', Sir Henry Lunn.

Anyway, when I left school, Mr. Hundleby took me on. I soon saw there was a lot to the job that the customer never saw! There was a deal of physical work for one thing. When someone asked for a pound of cheese we cut it with the wire and wrapped it but before this it had to be hauled in and skinned. 'Empire', a red Cheddar, was the ordinary cheese for a long time. Bacon, ham and shoulders came in Five-hundredweight boxes (N.B. 112 lbs = 1 cwt. = 50 kilos). They were in salt and had to be lifted out and washed in the copper boiler and then hung outside to dry. At night they were brought in and hung on hooks in the warehouse.

1 cwt. sacks of flour had to be weighed up into 3½ lb. bags and sugar came in cumbersome 2 cwt. sacks and had to be measured into 2 lb. and 4 lb. thick, dark blue paper bags – 'sugar paper.'

Tea came in large chests, of course, and it was scooped into plain square wrappers of ½ lb. (225 g.) and 1 lb. (450 g.) and labelled. All the dried fruit – currants, raisins and sultanas – had to be carefully washed and cleaned before it was wrapped – there were no ready made packets of 'mixed fruit'!

One of the worst jobs was the pepper, which came in 1 cwt. drums and had to be divided into tiny 2 or 4 ounce containers! We had to be careful not to spill any produce when we measured it out and with pepper we had to have our noses covered!

Another time-consuming task was dealing with the treacle. It came in barrels, with a lever to allow it to run out into jars. Well, in cold weather, it used to run very slowly, so I often did something else while waiting . . . yes, on one occasion I forgot about it and it overflowed all over the brick floor! We had a job cleaning it up!

The hardest job of the year was when we had to get a cartload of salt from the station. We carried it into the shop – it was in 1½ stone lumps – and it had to be wrapped in newspaper and carried upstairs to be stored in the warehouse, ready for customers killing their pigs.

In the old days, biscuits used to be in large, glass topped tins, angled up from the floor so the customer could see the choice.

A lot of shelf space was taken up by jams and many of the old makes have gone now – 'jam and bread' was a filling, cheap and tasty snack in the days before everything had to be good for you and not fattening!

Some customers of those days were almost like friends but not everyone stayed here long. On Lady Day (5th April) we always wondered who would have gone, as farm labourers, for example, were often only employed for one year, which started on Lady Day.

I moved to the Woodhall Shop about 1925, when the manager was Mr. E. Robinson. Then I could do more things in Woodhall. I liked sport and I played football for the Woodhall Wednesday team. Footballs were made of leather and were laced up. Players could be cut from the laces when heading the ball. In summer I was always hoping that I could close the shop promptly so that I could dash home for my racquet and cycle to the tennis courts! They were where the bowling green on King George Avenue is now.

A favourite Sunday afternoon pastime was to sit on deck chairs listening to the band playing in the Bandstand, near the Spa Baths and Pump Room. In the Season it was interesting to see the customers and what they were wearing – smart city fashions and yet there were squirrels, red ones then, scampering about nearby.

Then there were always lovely walks. There used to be a very pretty one which went behind the Teahouse and Kinema and along the edge of Petwood grounds. There were beautiful shrubs and heathers there. Later – it was when they gave Jubilee Park to the village – the Weigalls railed it off.

There was talk that the Weigalls had intended to build a new Bath House before they left Woodhall, before they gave the park to the village. It was going to be where the café in the park is now but that didn't happen.

When they left Petwood they took the stone paving from the terrace (the raised strip across the garden, halfway down from the house). A horse and dray took it to the station to be put on the train. What a weight!

In winter there used to be dances in the Winter Gardens of the Royal Hotel, where Royal Square is today. Mr. Lee, the plumber, had the key – I think he had to see to the heating.

He lived where the chemist's shop is. His daughter, Maisie, married Russell Waterhouse and they ran the Bakery – nearly next door to her father – for many years. The Winter Gardens was a lovely place for dances, right in the middle of the village and beautiful inside with its potted palms and ferns. We had some happy times there.

I was married in 1932. My wife came from Louth and when she came to Woodhall Spa she worked as a waitress at the Spa Hotel. (Spa Court flats now). It took me back, gave me a strange feeling, when I rang the bell of number eight today – that was exactly where the French doors into the dining room of the hotel used to be and I would go there, to see her at work, seventy years ago! She didn't know Woodhall at all when she came and on her first day off, she decided to walk down Witham Road to get to the seaside! Fortunately, someone told her 'there's only the river down there, duck' before she had walked too far! At the time she worked there, Mr. Jervis was the hotelier at the Spa.

I was twenty minutes late for my wedding! It was Boxing Day and lovely weather for us to drive to Louth. Maurice Rose was my Best Man and had made the cake. His cousin, Cedric Wield, wanted to see a girl in North Somercotes, so we gave him a lift. Well, we got lost! There we were, somewhere in the Wolds with the cake, while the bride-to-be waited and thought there had been a mix up and the car wasn't coming to pick her up for church! Then, when we'd got to church the fan belt snapped! Cars weren't serviced regularly in those days – but what a start to a marriage!

After we were married we lived in a flat above the Royal Hotel, looking out onto Station Road with Bryant's shoe shop opposite. A niece of the Rose family was underneath and had a hairdressing business. We were great friends with her and used to go down there for baths.' (In 1932 bathrooms were not standard in flats or houses.) 'Later, Mr. Oyler bought that flat and came to collect the rent. My wife darned his socks for him – such holes! She put a big orange underneath to darn them. After a while Mr. Oyler and Mr. Millhouse bought the Abbey Lodge and started serving food there. Before that it had been a pretty rough and ready pub with corn shoved underneath the seats at harvest time'. N.B. Philip Oyler, M.A. Oxon., was an unusual innkeeper. He removed the bar and initiated a theatre at the Abbey Lodge and also introduced Tea Dances there. At the entrance to the inn was a notice, which was, no doubt, heartening for foreign visitors to the Spa but of limited interest to locals, 'Ici on parle français'.

'But back to myself and the shop, it was the year after we were married, in 1933, that my very good friend, Harold Howsam came as manager and we worked together until I was called up in 1940. I joined the Royal Artillery – H Ack Ack Regiment and was with it until I was demobilised, after three and a half years as Site Sergeant, in October 1945.

Of course, I still knew what was happening here during the war. There was that tragedy in 1941 when a car of local young men, including Clint Rose, went into the Drain and they all drowned. Mary Rose was at home with their toddler.

Then there were the parachute mines in 1943, one of which destroyed the Winter Gardens. Oh that was a shame but there was a tragedy too – Mr. Sleight of Cornwall Terrace was an Air Raid Warden and he was out, just on the bridge – at that time there was a footbridge over Tattershall Road – not two steps from his house, when the mine went off. He was all right but his wife and son, in the house, were both killed. Mrs. Overton, mother of Jack who had the greengrocer's shop, was injured; Dr. Armour's house was badly damaged too. Later Mr. Sleight married again – the sister of Bob Belton who was killed in action.

Mr. Hundleby died in 1945 and Mr. Howsam took over the Woodhall shop, where I joined him after demobilisation. Sadly his health deteriorated and he died when he was only 55, in 1958. After his death I managed the business for Mrs. Howsam – until I retired in 1974.

Retired from the grocery business but not from Woodhall Spa! This has been my home for over ninety years and if I let myself drift into memories there are so many people of the past

1928. L. Chapman standing at the right of the photograph.

Woodhall Spa Wednesday Football Team, 1928.
The team played on the Broadway Ground which was beyond the Golf Hotel.
V. Setchfield, S. Johnson, J. Overton, A. Robinson, J. Leary, L. Chapman, W. Baker,
H. Hudson, F. Mehen, F. Smith, Rev. Oxborough, V. Johnson, C. Rose.

. . . Rev. Benson Brown, Vicar of St. Peter's; Matron Greenshields at Alexandra Hospital; nurses Ward and Crooks; Mr. Pacey at the Post Office – we had two deliveries and two collections daily then; Miss Browning, the first matron at Fairlawns; Mr. Greenfield who cut the lawns at Petwood – his son was a gardener too and his daughter had a fruit shop on Station Road; Miss Lamb at The Eagle; Mrs. Sneath at Claremont and Mr. Hunter at Woodlands (Broadway Carpets) . . . oh, so many ghosts!

I've had a fortunate life. I think I've always tried my best – that's how we were brought up, isn't it? But it's nice when your work is recognised so I was very pleased, in 1961, when I was elected President of Lincoln and District Grocers Association. Then, in 1968 I was chosen as President of the East Midland Grocers Association. Through that I was invited to a National Grocers Federation private dinner party given by Baroness Phillips J.P. at the House of Lords. We were all shown round the House afterwards. I remember the date   I suppose it was a highlight for me – 27th January 1969.

Who would have imagined it? A little foundling boy from a small village out in the country, growing up to be entertained in the House of Lords and living to be over 90! Of course, there have been worries, disappointments and great sadness – we all have our share of those – but I think I have been lucky. I've had kindnesses and friendship from so many people and an interesting, happy life!'

Arthur Leggate
who was a member of the UDC in 1960

'Before the bridge over the Witham, when there was the ferry, barges, often called 'packets', were drawn up the river by horses. I know sugar beet from Leggate's farm, maybe 60 tons of it, was taken this way to the factory at Bardney. There was a pub, the 'Goose and Gridiron,' about where Mill and Green Lane are, which was used by river traffic. The river sometimes froze in winter. Once, Rose took bread to customers by pony and trap on the river. Their bakery lasted over 50 years although they stopped using the windmill well before the second World War. It had a steam engine so that mill could grind when there was no wind. 1947 was a very bad winter and people skated to Lincoln.'

Recorded memories of
Horace ('Joe') Hudson

'We came to live at 1 Cromwell Cottages, on Albany Road, Woodhall Spa, in 1907, when I was two. It was near the first golf course, off Tattershall Road and we used to find golf balls in the garden. Those old balls were called 'gutties'.

Mr. Fairburn was head of St. Andrews when I went to school. I remember the Weigalls asking him for half a dozen boys to be ball boys at Petwood – they often had crack tennis players staying. There was no netting around the court so it was jolly hard work but they were given 2s/6d (12½p) for the afternoon – that was money!

Oh, money's changed. Everyone talks of the wonderful train service but we couldn't afford to go to London. About the only outing we had was Whit Monday fun on decorated floats going around Woodhall Spa! I have receipts from my parent's furniture from Ray and Kemp of Horncastle dated 1902. They total £14 6s 10d and include 38 shillings for a couch, 15s 6d for a table and 1s 3d for a wash basin.

My father worked at Atkinson's Brewery, by the Railway Hotel, Kirkstead and he was in the Fire Brigade. Rockets used to be fired to summon the men. The fire engine and hose cart were pulled by horses supplied by Mr. Overton.

I left school at 13 – a year early but the family needed the money. I did all sorts – errand boy, paper round at 6 in the morning and evening work in hotels, gardening, anything! That was at the end of the 1st World War. There used to be training places for troops up in the woods behind the Kinema. They were older volunteers who hadn't been conscripted. They wore a different uniform and practised with wooden dummy rifles. Trenches were dug – at the bottom of Petwood gardens, all covered in brambles and such now.

It was very different in the Spa then. The Victoria Hotel was very grand and pretty from the outside. It had coloured glass candleholders to hang from the trees and in the pinewoods around the Kinema, in the Season. You could often hear the band playing as there were three bandstands. The big, military bandstand was near the Kinema and a smaller, pretty wooden one was in front of Doctor's Cottage at the side of the Baths, with deck chairs ranged round with their backs to the cottage. The third was on Victoria Avenue, which was open shrub land where there are bungalows now, opposite Doctor Robertson's house. Funny what you remember about the Season – I recall a cowboy, from London, riding down the Broadway, swinging his lasso! Perhaps he was a guest of the Weigalls.

Life was simpler when I was young. On Sunday evenings after church we would sing religious songs in each other's houses and then go home for a bite of supper. Sometimes Johnny Wield would take us home and show us the stars through his telescope. He seemed to know them all and got us really interested.

I played football for Woodhall Wednesday. We used to go to matches on pushbikes, with one on the crossbar – taking it in turn. I remember a match against Louth. We cycled there, in pouring rain, at 10am and played on little better than a swamp. We were trounced, partly because Louth, unfairly, had some 1st Division players in their team. We stayed on a bit in the evening and cycled home very late! Jack Overton, goalkeeper, had his thumbs bent back with the weight of the wet, leather ball and I don't think he played goalkeeper again!

We were a proper community then and Mr. Hotchkin was a real squire. I remember his 21st. It was a real village 'do' at the Manor House and the first time I had too much to drink! I was in trouble with my mother when I got home! People from the village used to go to the Manor House for help and justice if they had a problem. It was personal, not like today's telephone calls to officials you've never met. I know many things are better now but then we were a proper, caring community.'

Recorded reflections of
Ron Steadman, builder, born 1911

'My grandfather came over here in the late 1880s. He was a carpenter and could see the possibilities in Woodhall Spa for anyone connected with the building trade. He was right. He started a business and had enough work for himself and four sons.

After my grandfather's death, my father took over and I went into the decorating side so we could provide all aspects of the trade. The firm was Steadman Bros. and we built many properties, for example along Kirkby, Roughton and Mill Lanes, as well as doing general building work. In the event of a large job we sometimes worked with Arthur Kirkby. For example, we were in partnership for the gym and swimming pool at St. Hugh's. Later we did a lot of work for Mr. Forbes, at St. Hugh's, – such an enthusiastic gentleman.

During the war I was in the Royal Artillery and I was overseas on D-day. I had to make my way home through Normandy, Belgium and Germany to the Baltic. I arrived home at Christmas to find that my father had died three months before. Stafford Hotchkin and the local M.P. had got my brothers released to work in the business.

There are some interesting houses in Woodhall Spa. There are the ones designed by London architect Adolphus Came, with their distinctive timbering. Others are large and individually designed for wealthy people who have lived here. I remember a Mr. Clarke, who lived in 'Raftsund,' next to St. Hugh's School and Mr. Cannon, who had a glue business in Lincoln to which he was driven by chauffeur every day, from 'Fairmead' on Stanhope Avenue. An interesting story was that 'Longwood House,' on the corner of Iddesleigh Road and the Broadway, was designed to resemble Napoleon's dwelling when he was exiled on St. Helena.'

N.B. Time moves on. 'Raftsund' has for some years, prior to 2003, been part of St. Hugh's School, while 'Fairmead' is at present being redesigned as apartments. The only visible similarity between Longwood House and the building on St. Helena is an arched effect at the front. Otherwise they appear very different. However, they are both called 'Longwood House.'

The Alexandra Hospital. Opened in 1890 at a cost of £3,000.

Mrs. Wilkinson.

Hartington House School for Young
Ladies – The Misses Lunn,
Susannah, Katie and Florrie.

Miss Lunn's School 1903.

Cottage Museum Collection.

CHAPTER II

Mrs. 'Toby' Wilkinson and
Miss Lunn's High School for Girls

Mrs. Wilkinson, a lively and smartly dressed lady, has a beautifully furnished apartment in Kirkstead Court, Woodhall Spa. It would surprise people to know that she was born 96 years ago, in 1907.

This was just six years after the death of Queen Victoria and seven before World War I. Emmeline Pankhurst and the Suffragettes were employing nuisance tactics to gain women the vote. The two year old bus service in London, was gradually replacing thousands of horse-drawn vehicles, with double decker buses with solid rubber tyres. The Liberal Party, with Campbell Bannerman as Prime Minister, was governing the country. Keen on social reform, they introduced Old Age Pensions just one year after Mrs. Wilkinson's birth – an innovation which she has enjoyed for longer than most!

Christened Clarice Rose May but dubbed 'Toby' by the nurse when she was born, she spent her childhood in a farmhouse, 'North Drove Farm,' situated in the far-stretching fields across the River Witham, towards Martin Dales. No trace of it remains. One of a family of five, she was several years younger than her brothers and sisters, who had left school before she started. One of her brothers fought in World War I.

'He wrote to us, of course, but I was too young to understand properly, it was just like a story to me and life here was so quiet – oh, but I do remember a Zeppelin coming over! It was really bright moonlight and we saw it following the river. We ran out to look, just as we were but we got a dreadful shock when the bomb dropped. Then I realised my feet were hurting – nothing to do with the bomb but it was harvest time and I'd run out without my shoes so my feet were cut up from the stubble!' N.B. Zeppelin raids were reported in Lincolnshire in September 1916. The actual towns were rarely named but bombs are known to have been dropped along the River Witham. 'The other thing I remember is how sad we felt when they came for the horses, if they wanted them for the war. They just came and took them and we didn't get anything for them. On the farm they were well taken care of and it was awful to think of them being shot at, at the front.

There was no-one to take me to school so I didn't start until I was seven. Then I had to walk along the lengthy road to the bridge over the Witham. It was a very quiet road in those days, only an occasional pony and trap passed me.' Nowadays this lonely walk in all weathers would not be entertained for (or by) youngsters but, as Mrs. Wilkinson says, they were used to walking and there didn't seem to be the dangers then.

On reaching the river there would occasionally be the excitement of the bridge being opened to let a barge through. It was a toll bridge and it cost 1 penny to cross. On the other side was Kirkstead Station (now converted into a house) where Mrs. Wilkinson caught the train for the short journey into Woodhall. She then walked up the Broadway to Hartington House, home of Miss Lunn's 'Woodhall Spa High School for Girls'.'

In his 'Book of Horncastle and Woodhall Spa,' David Robinson relates that Miss Lunn's father was a chemist and grocer in Bridge Street, Horncastle and that in 1896 she opened a girls' school above the shop. Within two years the school moved to new premises, 'Castanea,' in West Street, where, in 1901, Susannah Lunn was joined by her sister Florence and a Miss Buchanan was appointed assistant mistress. The school continued to flourish and larger premises were found in Hartington House on the Broadway of neighbouring Woodhall Spa.

Miss Lunn's School, c. 1913.

Staff at Hartington House School in 1923 or 1924.

Cottage Museum Collection.

Like so much of this village, Hartington House was designed by London architect Adolphus Came. Again like so many buildings in the Spa it was a boarding house, catering for some of the hundreds of visitors who arrived each summer for the Season. Its position and size were ideal for a school.

There had been other private schools in the village, one headed by Miss Eno in 1876 and 'a school for delicate young ladies' in 1889. Mrs. Wilkinson speaks of Burwood House in her day. This was in Victoria Avenue and run by a Mr. and Mrs. Chandler and she was a pupil there for a short time before changing to Miss Lunn's.

Boys had been catered for in Ernest W. Stokoe's 'Clevedon House Preparatory School' until it became the Clevedon Club, then the Clevedon Hotel and, finally, renamed the Golf Hotel in the spring of 1921.

There was, of course, the National School for both sexes, which had opened in 1847. At the beginning of the 20th century attendances at some, country, boys Grammar Schools were declining. Horncastle Grammar School was no exception. There were 47 pupils on roll in 1892 but only 24 in 1902. A letter by 'Educationalist' in the Horncastle News of 8th March, 1902, blamed agricultural depression and the consequent movement of families to manufacturing centres, for this decline. The writer said that, because of the falling roll, the Governors of Horncastle Grammar School had decided 'neither rashly nor timidly,' to admit girls 'to the educational advantages provided by the endowment they hold in trust.' He said that 'in the spirit of the times' it was necessary to have a 'fuller interpretation' of the quotation that 'woman was created to be a helpmeet for man.' So, in September 1902, girls were admitted for the first time to this ancient seat of learning, under the Headship of Rev. A. G. Madge, M.A., L.L.D. They were promised 'small classes and individual attention' at a cost of £1 13s 4d a term, for children aged 8 to 14, £2 13s 4d a term for 14 to 16 year olds and £3 6s 8d a term if over 16.

Meantime, one week after 'Educationalist's' letter in the 'Horncastle News,' Miss Lunn wrote that her school for Junior girls was 'continuing under her personal supervision' in Horncastle. In this establishment careful attention was paid to 'laying the foundation of education and the cultivation of refined and ladylike manners.' A Kindergarten for 3 to 6 year olds would be opening after Easter. Advertisements in May gave Miss F. Lunn (Florence) as being in charge of the Junior Department of the High School, in the Masonic Hall, Horncastle and stated that 'The Misses Lunn will be at home on Thursdays.'

The older girls, 'more advanced pupils,' were to be provided with free rail tickets to Woodhall Spa, where they would be educated to Cambridge and London Matriculation standard. An advertisement described Hartington House as having its own grounds for tennis, croquet, etc. while there were large playing fields a short distance away for hockey, cricket, etc. Girls attending the school would have 'fresh air, good food and moderate exercise.' The fees were, reportedly 1½ guineas a term when the school first opened.

A third sister, Katie, had joined Miss Lunn as Matron at Hartington House and the school flourished, so that, after a while, neighbouring Victoria Lodge was acquired in order to accommodate more pupils. It too was a boarding house which had been run by Mrs. Huggins.

By 1915, when Mrs. Wilkinson was a pupil, Miss Lunn's High School for Girls was well established and had grown considerably. The following 'Education Announcement' (nothing so vulgar as an advertisement) appeared in the 'Horncastle News' in January:-

'Hartington House School Woodhall Spa
Principal Miss Lunn. Assisted by Miss Katharine Lunn, Certificated Nurse.
Miss K. M. Brooks, London Honours B.A., English & Modern Languages.
Miss R. A. Lord, London B.Sc., Maths, Physiology & Hygiene.
Miss M. E. Griffiths, L.R.A.M. Pianoforte, Harmony Class singing.

Miss E. M. Maynard, London, Matriculation, English & German.
Miss M. Rogers, Kindergarten, Swedish Drill & Games.
Mademoiselle Nusschler, Conversational French.
& also Visiting Professors.
Miss M. E. Edgar, Art Master's Certificate, Painting & Drawing. Wednesdays.
Miss Kathleen Jackson, Gold Medallist of Royal Academy of Music
Elocution. Fridays
Miss Rix. Mrs. Wordsworth's School of Dancing, London. Fridays.
Mr. F. Hughes, F.R.C.O., Solo singing & organ.
Mr. J. R. Hilton, Violin, 'Cello, etc. Mondays
The school reopens Tuesday January 19th at 10am.'

When Mrs. Wilkinson started at the school, in 1914, she remembers most of the pupils being boarders. Because of this and because of her late start she found it difficult to make friends at first. However, there were other farmers daughters like herself and she soon discovered that daygirls could be useful to the boarders. After school, at 4pm, before walking down to the station, she would cross the road to Poucher's, the Bakery opposite Hartington House (the Bakery and Delicatessen today) and buy the requested number of walnut whips! These were handed over to the eager boarders next day.

The three Misses Lunn were well regarded, she thinks. 'All spinsters' but that wasn't unusual with all the strong men away in the Forces. Susannah was known as 'Miss Sally' and was very much the Head, while the rather quiet Miss Katie was Housekeeper and Cook. Miss Florence gave piano lessons but Mrs. Wilkinson remembers being taught to play 'by an elderly gentleman – well, they all seemed elderly' she laughingly remarks. 'Miss Florence . . . I don't remember what she did particularly . . . I think she just floated about!'

Games were played in the afternoon – tennis, croquet and, perhaps surprisingly, archery and cricket. In June 1917 a tennis match was played between the school and Woodhall Spa Ladies. It was evidently an exciting match as the girl's team composed of Monica Escombe, Olive Farrow, Lesley Wintringham, Dorothy Golland, Mary Holmes and Kathleen Oldfield won by 37 games to 35. Then the return match was a draw at 36 games each.

'If the weather was wet or if we were practising for a concert we wouldn't have games. Sometimes the school was involved in village events, like that grand Pageant about the discovery of Spa water. That was in the Spa grounds before I started at Miss Lunn's.' (On this occasion in 1911, pupils from the school are reported as acting in a scene of druidical worship!).

'We had a concert for parents at the end of term, in the Royal Hotel Winter Gardens. it was lovely to go down there and no distance from the school, on the same side of the road . . . but in any case, there wasn't any traffic to speak of then.'

The school end of year concerts and prize-givings were obviously big events, meriting considerable coverage in the 'Horncastle News.' In 1909, Princess Marie Louise (friend of the Baroness von Eckhardstein, later Lady Weigall, of Petwood) gave the prizes. The following year, shortly before her marriage to Captain Weigall, it was the Baroness herself. She made an encouraging speech, quoting 'let those who will be clever.'

In 1915 there was a lengthy report on the 'Annual Prize Distribution' at which there had been 'an exceptionally large and distinguished gathering.' This year there was 'a small admission charge' in aid of the local Red Cross Hospital. The 'splendid entertainment' by the pupils was a performance of an operetta, Clementine Ward's 'Princess Ju Ju.' After a detailed description of the plot the reporter concluded that 'The rounds of applause for the singing and charm of the dancing reflected the highest credit on the teachers.' After the performance tea was served to the music of the Royal Hotel Band. Then came the prizegiving, with the recently appointed Canon Whiting in the chair. Miss Lunn announced that this year War Loan vouchers were being given as prizes and said how pleased she was to see soldiers 'who had so recently been fighting at the front', among the audience.

In July 1923 there was again a large gathering of parents in the Winter Gardens of the Royal Hotel for the Annual Prize Giving of Hartington House School. In a 'spirit of happiness' the girls performed 'Swineherd,' a play based on a Hans Christian Anderson story with Edith Eves, Dorothy Clements, Eva Wright and Mary Grist taking the main parts. The company then repaired to the garden of Hartington House for prizegiving, presided over by Lt. Col. Sir Archibald Weigall. In her report Miss Lunn claimed that the girls were taught to show initiative and resource and that their exam results had been excellent. Health had been good throughout the year and a Girl Guides troupe '1st Woodhall Spa Co.' had been formed. As she had done 13 years earlier Lady Weigall presented the prizes. In her enthusiastic and flamboyant way she said how happy she was to meet 'such a lot of brilliant girls.' They could always count on her as a friend. She had been Chief Guide of Australia during her recent time there and was thrilled to hear of the start of Guiding in Woodhall Spa. She urged the girls always to show gratitude and try to make the world 'a happier place for having passed that way.' Lady Weigall appealed to parents to meet the teachers. In Australia, she said, social parties were held for this purpose and at them 'hereditary gifts and weaknesses' could be discussed! In his speech Sir Archibald declared that England owed its greatness not to material wealth or possessions but to 'fine spirit and character carried all over the world.'

The speeches were followed by prize giving and afterwards Lawn Tennis Finals matches were played and there was an exhibition of work for parents to view. After tea there was a concert of both unison and solo singing and a performance of Rhythmic Dancing.

Occasions such as this were obviously splendid events but what of ordinary school life?

'Well, when we arrived in the morning we hung up our coats on the pegs – you had to make sure it was your peg! The school uniform was lovely. It was navy and gold and the blazer was very smart, navy with gold braid. We wore Boaters on our heads at first then, later, Panama hats came in. There is a photo of the girls before I started there and they are wearing skirts but I remember gymslips. They've gone out of fashion haven't they? You looked all right in a gym slip whether you were fat or thin and I dare say they didn't show the older girls figures too much – we were expected to look and act like well brought up young ladies – not that we always did!

The day began with Assembly before we divided into classes – about 15 in each I think and not strictly according to age. We sat in desks, in rows and listened to the teacher at the blackboard or we scratched away with pen and ink. There was an ink monitor who had to check inkwells were full before lessons started. We were taught all the usual things – the 3 R's, of course and History and Geography – there've been lots of changes in that since those days, so many places have changed their names. I don't think there was Science as such but we did Nature Study – birds and trees and looking at flowers. I'm afraid I wasn't academic; my reports usually said 'could do better'! But it didn't seem to matter – we just did what we could and the staff didn't bother too much. If you couldn't do something you were just told to close your book!

As well as being disadvantaged by starting school late I was very troubled during my first years by my mother's illness. She had several operations. There were chores for us to do at home and no-one to help or push me on with my schooling. Some of the girls went ahead though and passed university local exams.'

Examination results were published in the local newspaper. In 1918 it was reported that the school had been very successful in Senior, Junior and Preliminary examinations. In particular, J. Y. Marshall and F. R. Hanson had obtained a standard sufficient for exemption from Part II if they were to enter Girton or Newnham Colleges, Cambridge. The subjects for seniors were listed – English Composition, Scripture, Henry V, General Literature,

Cottage Museum Collection.

Hartington House School on The Broadway, Woodhall Spa.

Woodhall Spa on old picture postcards.

A group of Girls at Hartington House School, Woodhall Spa, taking part in the Pageant.

English History, French, Geography, Physical Geography, Arithmetic, Geometry, Algebra, Shorthand and Music.

Musical successes in examinations with the Royal Academy and Royal College of Music were also published. There were various pianoforte teachers over the years – Miss Griffiths, L.R.A.M. and Miss Smith, L.R.A.M. in the 1910s and Mr. Lawrence Richardson, organist of St. Peter's in the early Twenties. Successful girls included Zeta Hoot, Dorothy Golland, Doris Auckland – 'oh yes, my sister' excalaimed Mrs. Wilkinson, Winifred Kirkby and Rita Overton.

Rita Overton features in 1922 when she and Barbara Davis played the parts of the children in a scene 'King Charles bidding farewell to the children' which was part of a village pageant in aid of the Waifs and Strays Society. Miss Lunn, herself, also acted in this

Hartington House High School played its part in charitable work. During the war, in 1916, there was a performance of 'The Gitana,' a cantata for treble voices with dancing,' followed by a Sale of Work and 'various amusing competitions' in aid of Parochial Church Funds. Miss Lunn was evidently interested in music. A Woodhall Spa Choral Society was formed in the winter of 1921 and she was one of the committee. The first practice was held at the school. Just a few months before the end of the war, in April 1918, the school donated 'all kinds of good things' including tins of fruit, eggs, jam and cigarettes' to the Alexandra Hospital. On this occasion there were donations from other organisations, which gave, among other things, socks, pillowcases, books, pyjamas and, interestingly, <u>flags</u>.

Art, or at least 'Drawing,' also featured in reports of examination successes, with 45 out of 52 entrants, taught by Miss Edgar, passing the Royal Drawing Society's examination in July 1917, 35 of whom attained Honours.

Hartington House was used for lectures open to the public. In March 1916, a former curate of Horncastle, Rev. T. Dent, gave a talk on his internment in a German Prisoner of War camp. Less disturbingly, in June Rev. Canon Whiting lectured on Cathedrals and the following year there was a lecture 'Visions of Jeanne d'Arc from a psychological aspect.' This was different! Reading between the lines of the report one has the impression that the audience was a little bemused by the 'psychological aspect.' It is suggested that some preparatory reading would have been advisable! It is always good to hear of promotion. In May 1924, the erstwhile Canon Whiting of Woodhall Spa gave a talk about the island of Mauritius, of which he had become Venerable Archdeacon. A far cry from being Vicar of St. Peter's, Woodhall Spa.

Mrs. Wilkinson continued her description of the school day. 'At the end of the morning's work we were given lunch, cooked by Miss Katie. During the meal we had to talk in French, no English was allowed, so sometimes it was a rather silent lunchtime!

Discipline was fairly strict, we had to do as we were told. Sometimes we were 'told off' or given lines to write. you knew you were in trouble if you were sent to Miss Sally's study. That meant a serious reprimand and you had to stand and apologise and look very meek and contrite. Apart from the usual things like behaviour and talking in class and not working properly and not doing homework – oh, all the things children do, or don't do when they should! . . . apart from those they insisted on things which would never be considered now. For example, we always had to wear gloves outside, even to go the short distance from the school to the station. If we were seen without them there would be 100 lines to write 'I must at all times wear my gloves outside.' We always had to change our shoes when we went out – even to go to the Lodge next door. Mind you, I think that was to save their carpets!

After school was over for the day, at the end of the afternoon, I made sure I had what I needed for homework in my satchel, took my blazer off its peg, put my gloves on (!) and walked to the station. Sometimes, when I passed Woodlands, I'd see Mrs. Hunter in her wheelchair. She was taken to the Clinic for treatment by Mr. Wield, sometimes pulled by his donkey. Mr. and Mrs. Hunter had Woodlands as a boarding house.

Once on the train I sat next to a friend who had travelled on it from Horncastle, from the Grammar School. Sometimes she helped me with my homework, although there wasn't much time between the two stations!

Then it was across the bridge and the lonely walk home, between the fields, to the farm. It was lovely in summer sunshine, before the harvest. I wasn't much higher than the corn at first! But sometimes the wind nearly blew me over, with nothing to stop it blowing across the fen. In winter it was a bit ghostly in the quiet dusk and moonlight.

I don't often think of those early days, they seem part of a different time. We were very contented with family life and friends. Woodhall Spa was lovely then with private shops and windows full of pretty things, like Miss Parkin's, at the Crossroads, with beautiful needlework. The Teahouse was lovely when I was a girl. The Misses Williams who ran it, came from London every year for the Season. They wore mauve dresses and white aprons and picture hats. There were pretty tablecloths and the china was patterned with violets and everything was served so nicely. Squirrels scurried round the tables and there were lots of birds in the trees round about. I think the appeal of the Teahouse was that everything was so elegant in a natural rustic setting.

The High School for Girls was part of this village life. I think the school was well thought of and there was a society for past pupils.' An Old Girls Reunion was reported in June 1914. The weather was fine and 'the delightful grounds of Hartington House at their best.' There was a tennis tournament continuing, 'with great zeal,' all day, the winners being Miss J. Chapman and Miss L. Talbot. Lunch and tea were served in the school and Miss Lunn was thanked for allowing the 'now well established' association to meet there again.

The enterprising Miss Lunn had an even more entrepreneurial brother. He became Sir Henry Lunn of Travel Agency fame. It was Sir Henry who gave the prizes at the end of the school year in 1924. The Vicar of St. Peter's, Rev. Benson Brown, spoke of his boyhood friendship with Sir Henry with whom he had attended school. Sir Henry exhorted the girls not to look upon study as 'drudgery.' He spoke of the 'romance of figures,' not only in Mathematics but also related subjects such as Astronomy. There was the usual long list of examination, musical and drawing successes, with the names of prize winners such as Dulcie Howell, Gladys Laughton-Smith and Gabrielle Cotton-Smith, evocative of a different age.

Miss Lunn retired from her High School for Girls at Easter in 1926. She was succeeded by Miss Joaquim, B.Sc. who, later moved the school to 'Fairmead' in Stanhope Avenue, before that became part of St. Hugh's Preparatory School.

Hartington House reverted to being a Guest House. Miss Lunn continued to live in Woodhall Spa, with Florence and Katie, for 30 years until her death. Described as 'a born optimist,' she died in Lincoln County Hospital just after her 90th birthday, at the beginning of August 1956.

Miss Lunn's successful High School for Girls maintained its standards through the national events of the first quarter of the Twentieth century – the Edwardian age, World War I and the lead up to the General Strike, which began a month after her retirement. There had been also many local changes since the school opened here. The Golf Course had been made, the village had declined as a spa, the prestigious Victoria Hotel had been destroyed, the Concert Pavilion had become the Kinema. Mrs. Wilkinson smiled, reminiscently. 'Oh yes, so many changes, well we have to be prepared for those and I think Miss Lunn's did that – prepared girls for life as well as educating us. Yes, a well regarded establishment in a prosperous village but, for myself, well, my childhood perhaps – but I couldn't say that my schooldays were the happiest time of my life!'

Arthur and Joan Houldershaw

Arthur's grandfather lived at the big house, 'Darwood,' at Old Woodhall but, somehow, he says, the money disappeared.

Arthur was the eldest of ten children and, as sometimes happened, he was sent to live with an aunt so that there was one less to look after and feed at home.

'I left St. Andrew's School at 14, to work in Rose's bakery. I worked a 60-hour week for 10 shillings. It was hot work and I developed health problems, from the fumes stoking the furnaces. I was unable to fight in the 2nd World War because Dr. George Armour had found out I had ulcers.

I got a job driving lorries. I didn't sit a driving test for a licence, as it wasn't necessary then. I drove for Harvey's, farmers at Coningsby, taking cattle all over England. There was a 20 miles per hour speed limit and I was once fined for doing 27mph but, luckily, it wasn't put down. Often when I arrived at the delivery point the watchman wasn't there to take the load and I'd find him in the pub! Sometimes in the cities, like Birmingham, there was dense smog and they had covered flares on the pavement so people could see where they were going and where the kerb was. I also remember seeing ladies eating black pudding in the street, having taken knives for the purpose out of their handbags!

In Woodhall I remember the gas lighter going round. There weren't as many lamps as the electric streetlights we have now and they were only on the main roads.

Coal was delivered weekly, in sacks that were piled on a horse drawn cart. All the cooking at home was done on the big, black-leaded, kitchen range, heated by the coal fire. In the range there was a boiler compartment and water was poured in to be heated. Baths were taken in front of the fire. If we needed water upstairs it had to be carried up.

Shops have changed frequently over the years. When we were lads there was Hopps ice-cream at the crossroads, near Mrs. Tyler, who sold sweets. She also had cups and things for picnics in Jubilee Park, it was before the café there was built. On Station Road there was Fatty Burns ice cream parlour. He made his own ice cream. Of course, there weren't freezers full of ice cream like we find in supermarkets now. At Overtons greengrocery, on Tattershall Road, everything was in sacks, very fresh and good quality. Once, a chap called Lawrence Major worked there. Poor lad, his mother had poisoned his father. The crime was discovered after Mr. Major died, when the dog was given some of the poisoned food. Mrs. Major was the last woman to be hanged in Lincoln. The Post Office was where it is now but only doing Post Office business, not selling things and the telegraph boy stood outside. We enjoyed the circus when we were young. It came twice a year to a field with two old railway carriages, behind where the fire station is now.

I married Joan in 1948 and we came to this bungalow. It cost £1,400. At the bottom of the garden was a field (where Tor-o-Moor Gardens is now) and we rented part of it and kept chickens there!'

Joan was also one of ten children but she was the second youngest. Her father was a blacksmith in Coningsby. 'I remember Woodhall shops, too', says Joan. 'There were a lot of dress shops – Mrs. Kent and Mrs. Long and Miss Orpen if you wanted something special. There was also, a dressmaker, Miss Blanchard.

Year after year we used to come to Petwood to hear the Dagenham Girl Pipers. It was a treat but every year the same thing!

Many people were in service in Woodhall Spa. I knew someone who had half a day off a week and had to be in at 9 each night. Her wage for the week was 5/- and her first week's money went to pay for false teeth for her mother!

Aristocratic lady in a donkey drawn chair.

Taking the air in the grounds of the Victoria.

Asenath, Cedric and Effie Wield.

The picnic.

J. Wield, Cottage Museum Collection.

During the war there were a lot of Poles here and Sister Lewis at the Home for Gentlewomen – she was wonderful with her ladies – married one. Apparently he was a baron in Poland but here he just worked for the forestry but Sister Lewis liked to be called Baroness anyway!

We learned to make do with things during the war. The blackout material you had to buy for curtains could be bleached and then dyed for clothes and people made underwear from parachute silk. Of course, ordinary material was rationed, if you could get it. You were supposed to take the blackout very seriously and knock on a window if you saw a chink of light – sometimes people weren't pleased!

The Misses Lunn lived in Tarleton Avenue. It was rather odd that one was a Christian Scientist while Florence was church organist! Everyone was more aware of religion then. Not many people know that the name of the guesthouse, 'Oglee,' on Stanhope Avenue, is an acronym for 'Our God Loves Everyone Everywhere.'

The Hotchkins did a lot for the village. Colonel Hotchkin was generous to employees and there was always a parcel on the doorstep at Christmas. After their daughter, Faith, died, jewels from her rings were put round a chalice in St. Peter's. Of course her brother, Neil, is still alive. He's done such a lot to put Woodhall on the map with the golf course. Like his father he has been generous and caring towards people working for him and, even though times have changed, there has been a commitment to Woodhall Spa.'

Recorded memories of Cedric John Wield,
who lived at 'The Bungalow,' Iddesleigh Road,
now the Cottage Museum

'My grandparents came from Hampshire and they started working at the Baths in 1880. In 1884 they were put in charge and my grandfather was responsible for drawing up the water from the well while my grandmother organised baths for women.

In 1887 our bungalow, manufactured by Boulton and Paul, was provided for my parents by Mr. Hotchkin and the Medical Officer of Health and it was in that year that the bath chair business began. We had both donkey and hand drawn chairs. They were very necessary for taking ill or arthritic patients to the Baths but they were also used to transport people to the station or for outings for pleasure. The chairs had a door at each side with a footstool to facilitate climbing in and out. There was a soft leather apron to cover the legs and a hood, like a pram, for wet or windy weather. We had a forge with a fan driven fire, at the rear of the garden and a workshop, so my grandfather was able to shoe the donkeys and also make some of the chairs himself.

My father, John or Johnny as he came to be known, was born in 1877, and he married in 1898. He was a whitesmith with Humphersons, the ironmongers and sanitary engineers, which later became W. A. Dickinson's motor and engineering company. Mr. Dickinson was mother's brother.

I was born in 1908 and my sister, Effie, 4 years older than me, my parents and grandparents all lived in the bungalow. From being small children we had jobs to do and I had to polish the harnesses and brasswork on the bath chairs and groom donkeys – they were our pets, of course and they were stabled in the garden. At first we had no running water, there was a pump in the kitchen and a filter for drinking water. There were two earth closets outside the bungalow. For light we had oil lamps and candles to take to bed.

Accompanying Mother to the Baths for her treatment.

J. Wield, Cottage Museum Collection.

The Tea House.

Outside our front gate was a stereoscopic peep show which my grandfather had made. It needed 1d to operate and there were several scenes on a revolving drum. He also made violins out of sycamore. In fact, he made one the year he died, 1917, when he was eighty!

Visitors I met were always very kind and sometimes gave presents such as books and once I was sent several ducks and a drake, which roamed, around the garden!

After schooling here and at Horncastle Grammar School I became a Junior Clerk for the London and North Eastern Railway, at Woodhall Station. After that I was away a lot and married in 1935, so then I saw little of Woodhall Spa but my parents were still in the bungalow.

My father had many interests and could turn his hand to anything. Photography was a great interest and he had a dark room in the garden and he made cameras. He also gave magic lantern shows. He finished with the bath chairs when Nancy, the last donkey, died. By then there was little demand, as there were far fewer visitors to the Spa. He had become very interested in optics and this proved another source of income, as eventually, his prescriptions were accepted by the NHS and a room of the bungalow became the NHS office for the village. In view of this it was particularly cruel that my mother was blind for the last five years of her life. She died, aged 83 in 1961 and my father was 87 when he died three years later. Thus the Wield family were very much part of the growth, heyday and development of Woodhall Spa.'

Recorded memories of Mrs. Kathleen Wood
whose grandfather, Tom Hall, built the brick wall down the shaft of John Parkinson's coal mine.

My family lived at Reed's Beck. My father sometimes spoke of the changes which started with John Parkinson's digging for coal. Everyone was hoping to make money from the mine, of course. Nobody knew about the water or thought of the village of Woodhall becoming nothing, while a new Woodhall Spa developed.

My father was also called Tom Hall and his was the first khaki wedding (in army uniform) in St. Peter's Church. That was in 1917.

I was born in 1920. My father helped to cart stuff away from the Victoria fire that year. He said some of the helpers didn't do much after they discovered the hotel's alcohol!

We lived in several places round here. The quaintest was known as 'Teapot Hall', on the Boston Road near Scrivelsby. It was really small, just two rooms and what was called cruck built – the thatch came nearly down to the ground. When approached from Horncastle, a tiny bay at one side looked like a spout and the window opposite was the handle. People came to see the house because it was so picturesque but it was awful inside, so smoky and dark because of the trees. It burned down on V.J. night in August 1945.

Chapman's at the crossroads.

The store when it had become Kirkby's.

Cottage Museum Collection.

CHAPTER III

Recollections of an elderly resident

Gerald, as I shall call him, was born on 15th April 1913, when George V was King and Lloyd George, Prime Minister. The Labour Party had been in existence for three years. In 1913 steam power was opening up the country with more and more people striving to take the train to the seaside. Cars were mingling with carriages in London streets and aircraft had been seen in the sky. There was unease in the Balkans over Austrian domination and the economically strong Germany was arming itself at an alarming rate.

In England, 'Tango Teas' were the latest craze for Society hostesses. Special gowns were designed for these, such as one designed by Lady Duff Cooper ('Madame Lucille' of the fashion world) which was, daringly, slit at the back, almost up to the knee.

It is doubtful whether Tango Teas were held in Woodhall Spa, Lincolnshire but thousands of society folk came here, to the Spa Baths, during the April to October Season, hugely increasing the resident population of some fifteen hundred people.

'Yes, Woodhall Spa was quite small then' says Gerald 'I was born here and have lived here all my life. We lived in a house with stabling, which my parents had built. My grandfather was a pioneer of early potato growing. He was a member of the first Urban District Council here, when it was created in 1898. In fact, both my grandfather and my father served on the Council.

When I was a boy, Chapman's store was at the crossroads. It was well known and sold quality produce.'

The grandly named 'Chapman & Son, London & Manchester Stores. Est. 1845' sold grocery products but also crockery, millinery and various household goods. They advertised themselves as being 'suppliers to boarding houses, hotels, clergy and gentry.' They stocked hams from Denmark and Canada as well as some which were cured at Mareham le Fen, 'choice Colonial Cheddar cheese,' many biscuits, many teas, including their mysteriously named, 'Famous Self-Drinking Tea,' which, they claimed, was sent all over the country, and coffee which was freshly ground every day in the store.

'After Chapman's I remember a chap called Cargill,' Gerald continued. 'He ran a country delivery round for a while, before the shop became Kirkby's – Basil Kirkby selling clothing. His brother was a builder in the Spa. After Kirkby's, about in 1950, Penningtons took over – that was before they opened their clothes shop in Louth.

There were three bakers which I remember. Harness was on Witham Road and Rose was where the Pizza place is now, on Station Road. Their bakehouse was at the mill at the end of Mill Lane. Then there was Pouchers on the Broadway. They had a café for light meals and sold sweets, as well as bread, rolls and cakes, etc.

Two butchers I remember were Goodyear, on Witham Road, and Bourne, on the Broadway. They shared a slaughterhouse on Alexandra Road.

There was a fish shop, selling wet fish and fish and chips, on Witham Road, near the crossroads and there was Otters, another fish and chip shop further along the road.

Bryants shoe shop was on Station Road for many years, Forsters was a drapers next to the Post Office and Coney, on the Broadway, was a tailor, also selling quality makes of clothes as well as his bespoke tailoring.

Achurch, ironmongery, was on Tattershall Road, Dunhams on Station Road, sold furniture and china and Overton's House Agency was in the narrow, wedge-shaped shop next to the station – it was that shape because of the station platform.

There were two chemists for a while. The oldest was on Iddesleigh Road, opposite the Methodist chapel. At first this shop was in a very good position for customers from the Victoria Hotel and the Baths but after the Victoria went up in flames and less people used the Baths, it wasn't so central and Mr. Wokes moved to the premises on the Broadway.

As well as shops we had the usual trades people and cobbler, sweep, Mr. Daft the coalman, Mr. Gladwin the plumber – the village was pretty self sufficient. On the corner of Station Road and Tattershall Road was the Royal Hydro Hotel and Winter Gardens. R. A. Came, the architect who built it, arrived here with his company and stayed on to build half the village! Station Road was 'the Mall' when he built the Royal because of the shops he had there, although they weren't altogether a success. Came and others felt the Winter Gardens would attract visitors out of season. They were prefabricated in Germany and then the metal crossbars were cut to size in the blacksmith's here – on Witham Road, opposite where the Fire Station is now. The Royal was successful and after Came struck a new well, off Tattershall Road, he built a Bath-house. That was on part of what is now the Mall car park and over part of the present Royal Square. The Winter Gardens were pretty, decked out with palms and ferns and small tables. Many functions were held there, shows, tea dances, musical events – Dame Nellie Melba sang there once, when she was a guest of the Weigalls. Often there were money raising dances for societies and sports clubs, or the Alexandra Hospital.

Further up the road from the Royal was the Eagle. That had been built as a house by the Blytons, in about 1870, I believe and it looks much the same today. They owned a lot of land around the station and had a nursery up what is now Spa Road. After Blytons the nursery was Bishops, then Huggins and then Overtons.

The best hotel was the Victoria, behind the Broadway shops, near the Spa Baths. The Spa would never have been so popular without it. Spa Road wasn't there then and there were no houses there. The hotel had been a posting house at first. It had impressive entrance gates across from the railway gates from Iddesleigh Road. I was only just seven when it burned down. It was on a Sunday, the 4th April 1920. I knew about the fire early. Father had, in fact, just retired from being Captain of the Fire Brigade but he was called out and I woke up when he returned in the early hours. He said everyone desperately had done what they could, as they all knew what a disaster it would be if the place burned down but there just wasn't enough water to put it out. He was frustrated as well as shocked because he said that everybody had known that water would be a problem, if a fire started. I don't know why they didn't have a lake in the grounds, which they could have used against fire – they had just about everything else there – tennis, croquet, a bandstand, shrubberies and walks . . .

As well as the Victoria, Royal and Eagle there was the Goring Hotel, which became Lawson's during World War I. Goring was German and he had to leave the country after war started. The hotel became the Spa in the Twenties, when I was at school. Spa Court flats are there now.

Also there was the Clevedon. That had been Ernest Stokoe's boys school and then a club for gentlemen, run by his brother. The Stokoes had a lot to do with the Golf Club. The Clevedon became the Golf Hotel in about 1920.' (N.B. The bungalow next to the Golf Hotel is named 'Clevedon.')

'Apart from hotels there were numerous boarding houses and apartments. They were opposite the Golf, along Iddesleigh Road, Victoria Avenue, Cornwall Terrace, King Edward Road, oh everywhere.

The Teahouse was there when I was a boy. It was run by the Misses Williams who used to come up to Woodhall for the Season, each year. They bought the place outright about the time I was born, I believe.

W. A. Dickinson, Motor and Cycle Engineer.

Cottage Museum Collection.

The petrol pump by the roadside.

It was the railway that made the Spa. It was a really good through service from London. The company would lay on special trains for events here and occasions such as the Woodhall Show and Sports so that people would be able to stay to the end.'

The Lincoln to Boston railway opened in 1848 but it was the making of the branch line from Kirkstead to Horncastle, in 1855, which gave a boost to the Spa. It was, indeed, an efficient service with summer and winter services announced in the newspaper. '20th September 1924 Winter train times – Kings Cross to Woodhall Spa 4pm – 7.22pm and Woodhall Spa to Kings Cross 9.27am – 1.05pm' (so approximately 3½ hours).

However, motor transport caught on quickly as wealthy visitors began to arrive in chauffeur driven cars. 'Yes, Mr. Fuller had a garage on Witham Road and Mr. Dickinson had a cycle, motor and engineering shop where Laura Fowler's dress shop is. When I was very young Mr. Dickinson ran a charabanc for a while to take people about and to the seaside. It would hold about a dozen people and cost a few shillings. It was stored in his garage, where Budgens is. In front of his shop on Station Road he had a petrol pump, right at the edge of the pavement. That would certainly not do now with the amount of traffic there is. At least there is a pedestrian crossing now. That was suggested one Christmas time, over forty years ago but it was not considered necessary.

There have always been lots of clubs and societies in Woodhall Spa. All the sports, of course – tennis, cricket, football, croquet, archery and golf. The present Golf Course was well established before World War I, although it didn't become nationally well known until the Twenties. There were fishing matches on the Witham and a Cycling Club with Mr. S. V. Hotchkin as President, started just before World War II.

This being an agricultural area, there have been several Shows. Horncastle held its 'Annual Rural Fete' on Bank Holiday Mondays and Tattershall had a 'Foal Show and Sheep Fair' each year, in and around their market place – that was all grass then. There were stalls and roundabouts and skittles and sideshows and sales of drove horses and sheep. The Foal Show was in a field nearby. In Woodhall there was an 'Annual Show and Sports' before the First World War, with horses and bicycle races. Some competitors came from other counties, it wasn't just a local affair. That stopped in 1915 – the 1914 Show was held before war was declared. The Show was revived after the war and my father was secretary for it then. It was mainly athletics and bicycle races. The Agricultural Show proper started after the Weigalls had handed over Jubilee Park to the village in 1947 and was an annual event for fifty-two years. At one time, everybody went to the show, but ideas change and there is much more choice of activities these days and cars in which to travel to other events.

Father was also secretary of the Conservative Club which had a good membership. Whist Drives were popular there, not so much Bridge was played in those days. I remember there used to be Whist Drives to raise money for an ambulance. You know, in some ways we were better off then. I mean, if you broke your leg, there was an ambulance here to take you to the Baths where there were doctors and X-ray equipment – you didn't have to wait, then go all the way to Lincoln and wait when you got there.

Over the years there have been dramatic societies and music clubs and choirs here. By the way, St. Peter's Church had a very good boys choir at one time. Sometimes a religious play would be performed in St. Peter's – that was before the church hall was built. I remember a Nativity play in about 1930, which was performed on four evenings with the church full each night. I can still see the wonderful costumes of the three kings – just hessian but painted with bright colours and gold. The play was produced by Miss Joaquim when she had the school at Fairmead and we went for fittings there.

It's such a pity they pulled down the old St. Andrew's Church. It was considered to be unsafe from the effect of the 1943 land mine, when they demolished it, in 1957 but I think, nowadays, conservationists would be trying to find a way of propping it up. It seems so

St. Andrew's Church which was demolished in 1957.

The interior of St. Andrew's Church.

Woodhall Spa on old picture postcards.

strange to have the graveyard there, at the crossroads, without the church. Some of the stone St. Andrew's was built with came from Stixwould Priory. Inside it was white and there were ten carved angels looking down on the pews.

On the whole, we were a very country community in the early years of the twentieth century and the season visitors could almost have come from another world. I don't think local folk thought World War I was going to happen. I was only a year old but I've heard the story so many times. My Uncle Frank was in the Woodhall Spa branch of Horncastle Territorials and they knew they were to be called up immediately, if anything happened. The Declaration of War was announced from the bandstand of the Victoria Hotel. It was a big bandstand; suitable for accommodating a military band and the famous Black Dyke Band was playing. This was at the beginning of August and there were hundreds of visitors in the Spa. Ladies in beautiful gowns, with large, fashionable, hats and parasols and smartly suited men, carrying canes, were strolling through the gardens of the Victoria and listening to the band. Then it stopped playing, the fact that we were at war was solemnly declared and it was announced that the Territorials had to go immediately. You can imagine the drama and panic. Later, they were told it was to be the following morning. So the next day they marched to the station, with a crowd of well-wishers and the Black Dyke Band. I was told the atmosphere was of excitement and cheering rather than fear and foreboding. They didn't know what they were going to. At the station, the band played 'Auld Lang Syne' and 'God Save the King,' as the train steamed out, with everyone waving. My Uncle Frank did not return. He was killed at Boulon Wood in 1917.'

Many more men were killed in the 1st World War than the second. Names of victims of World War I are written in two columns on the War Memorial at the crossroads here. There are twenty-two. The names of the nine killed in World War II are written horizontally below. The Alexandra Hospital was used for wounded soldiers during the first war and Petwood for convalescents. The Weigalls opened up Petwood gardens with a small charge, for the war effort and Captain Weigall organised a Home Defence Corps.

'I remember the celebrations for the signing of the armistice in 1918. I had been in bed with 'flu for several days. There was an epidemic. It was the same 'flu that killed thousands of soldiers in the trenches. They reckoned that if you survived three days you would be all right. Well, I was O.K., although I caught pneumonia shortly afterwards, which left me with a patch on the lung – a serious matter then. But to get back to the eleventh of Novemer 1918, I was allowed up, out of bed, to look out of the window to see all the bunting and flags and all the people about. It had been declared a national holiday and all the schools were closed. The bells of St. Peter's rang for a long time. There was a united service there, I believe, in the evening, with hymns like 'O God our help in ages past.'

I didn't start school until I was eleven. It was the National school, just round the corner from me – the building is still there, it became the Garden Centre and now is the house at the front of Came Court on Witham Road. Some children, including 5 year olds, had to walk two or three miles. Several came from Reed's Beck. They were sent home half an hour earlier in the winter. Some children wore cut down trousers and tattered shirts with odd sleeves added – some families were very poor in those days before national assistance. Mr. Thompson was headmaster. He followed Mr. Fairburn who'd been there 27 years and was well respected. There were about 140 on roll and every morning the attendance figure was put up on the wall.'

Attendance was evidently very important and the week's figures, average and percentage were written in the school log book each week. The number of teachers and quantity of materials provided depended on these figures. There were regular visits from the Attendance Officer ('Kid Catcher') who rounded up truants. Children nearing 14, the school leaving age then, often did a bit of work before they'd left and there were always several away at potato picking time, in October.

Victoria Hotel.

Victoria Hotel.

Cottage Museum Collection.

'Oh yes, it was important for the family that children started earning as soon as possible and several did jobs while they were at school. One lad had a milk round and cycled round the village with a bucket on each handlebar. The measure hung inside the pail and people came out of their houses with jugs for their milk. He was about 12, I think. The school was closed when there was an important competition at the Golf Club. It was accepted that a lot of lads would be ball spotting and caddying and there might be no school for three or four days. One year, a girl called Ivy Roberts passed for the Grammar School – we had the scholarship exam and usually there were two or three who got through each year – but Ivy's parents wouldn't let her go. It would have cost a little but, I think, it was more that they needed her to start work – go into service, I think. I never sat the Scholarship. They made a mistake about my age and then I was too old. Imagine the fuss if that happened now! There was another boy who didn't seem particularly clever but he had perfect pitch. There wasn't a note Miss Rose could play on the piano without him knowing what it was. Such a gift. He ended up working on the land somewhere.'

Looking at the logbook it is surprising how often the school was closed for a day. There were national events such as the wedding of the Duke of York and Elizabeth Bowes Lyon (the late Queen Mother) in 1923 and local affairs such as the Woodhall Spa Athletic Sports, Kirkstead Sports, the annual Sunday School and Choir trip to Skegness and elections for the Urban District Council. Then there were the epidemics. In the Twenties the Medical Officer of Health was called in when several children were absent with an infectious disease and he decided whether the school should be closed. There were closures of a fortnight for Whooping Cough, Chickenpox and Measles and in the autumn of 1928 there was no school for six weeks because of an epidemic of Diphtheria. Immunisation against Diphtheria was undertaken in school in 1938.

'In my time I remember children being excluded because of Measles and Mumps and occasionally for dirty heads. But what with this and children not attending in bad weather, there could be a good third of the school absent. They started a school bus for the Reed's Beck pupils in about 1930. The School Dentist used to come into school to give treatment for a couple of days. It meant a bit of reorganisation of the classrooms but there was often a bit of shuffling about. If a teacher was absent, the classes had to be shared out – there wasn't always a supply to come in. Luckily, the Head's wife was a teacher so she could leave the housework and come in sometimes.

There were four rooms in the building with brick walls and a lot of green paint. The big room had a fire at each end – one was a slow combustion stove – but the place was often rather cold. Of course, we weren't used to central heating anywhere in those days. We were mixed age groups in each class and sometimes, if we had enough teachers, two classes would share a room.'

The following is taken from the log book, dated September 17th 1923, 'Two teachers have left the staff since March 29th and as no new appointments have been made the work of the school is being carried on with difficulty. There are 41 Infants under an uncertificated teacher. Std. I, II and III are under the Certificated Teacher. There are 60 children in these three standards.' The Headmaster took the remaining 52, older children. There was another uncertificated teacher by the spring of 1924 but it seems large mixed age classes and unqualified staff were usual.

'Being a Church School we went to St. Andrew's or St. Peter's quite often – Ash Wednesday, Maundy Thursday, Ascension Day and we had Diocesan Inspectors coming to school when we had to recite the Catechism and answer questions. We had a short memorial service at The War Memorial, at 11 o'clock on 11th November each year. The first time I went, it was only six years after the Armistice when the 1st World War ended. All the religion didn't stop us from misbehaving sometimes and then we might be caned – three blows on each hand.

Victoria Hotel.

Woodhall Spa on old picture postcards.

Victoria Hotel.

Cottage Museum Collection.

It was enough to draw blood and it was difficult to write afterwards or to hide it from your parents when you got home!

The boys did gardening at school. There were several plots with two boys to each plot. Every home had a garden, of course, and it was important we should know how to grow vegetables – no, no flowers. I think this is the right order for the vegetables – broad beans, potatoes, peas, carrots, cabbage and radishes and lettuce. They had prizes and one year when I came second I should have won. That year something new called 'camphorite' came out for protecting peas. Well, it didn't work. I should have used cotton as usual. The birds got my peas.' The prizes amounted to 10/- for the winner, 7/- second and 5/- third prize – quite a lot of money then.

'While we gardened the girls did needlework. They needed to know how to mend and alter clothes, turn collars and cuffs and such like.'

Visits from Mr. Murray to inspect the gardens are regularly noted in the log book. In 1922 he was the 'Gardening Inspector.' By 1927 he was dubbed the 'County Horticultural Instructor' and, still going strong in 1938, he had become the 'Horticultural Adviser to the Lindsey County Council.'

'Yes, we saw some people often – the Vicar and nurse for example – but there were unusual visits too, like the time we heard a wireless broadcast, that caused a great deal of excitement.'

The log book entry states, 'April 4th 1924. This afternoon, a local tradesman, Mr. B. Kirkby, fitted up a wireless installation in the school and at 3pm the children listened to Sir Henry Walford Davies, Director of Music to the University of Wales, who broadcasted to many schools in the London area the first wireless talk to children in their classrooms. The experiment was carried out by means of a loud speaker which was brought into the school and everything was heard very distinctly, including the musical illustrations.'

'1924 was still early days for wireless. Some of us had crystal sets at home – they were quite easy to make actually if you had the right bits.

I remember the General Strike of 1926. There were no newspapers for the first week or so and Mr. Dickinson had loudspeakers fixed outside his premises on Station Road to relay the latest news. Many bookings were cancelled here and I think every business suffered. There were proper metal roads in the village, when I was a boy, but not outside it. Kirkby Lane wasn't made up intil the twenties and Tor-o-Moor Road was much later than that. Before tarmac was put down roads were just wide paths of earth, gravelled over and steam rolled.

There used to be a stench pole in the centre of the crossroads. It was from when sewage was put in. Sewage disposal was a bit of a problem for the U.D.C. with so many summer visitors. Another problem and expense was the extending of the water supply to the outlying parts of Woodhall, such as down Witham Road to Kirkstead. The reservoir was along Kirkby Lane, on the right hand side just past Wellsyke Lane, going towards Kirkby on Bain.

Of course, Woodhall Spa was all about water. I've always thought the benefits of spa water would have been publicised much earlier if anyone important had taken notice of things people said. They used to say that water used to collect in a dip in Stixwould Road and drovers driving cattle along noticed that, however hot the weather, animals wouldn't drink from it. The drovers themselves found comfort from it for their aches and pains. Later there were plenty of springs about because lots of folk were digging down for coal – it wasn't just Parkinson who had that idea. Local men said that Came knew where to dig for a spring by following a line of melted snow, one occurs at the top of Spa Road. That idea is discounte- nanced by scientific people now but men who worked on the 1905 well – and they were all local, not professional men – were sure of it. One of them worked for us when he was an old man and he often spoke to us about it. As well as striking spa water near the Royal, Came also dug successfully in Arnhem Way. The water from these two wells was supposed to be even better than at the Baths but there was less of it.

Royal Hotel.
Woodhall Spa on old picture postcards.

Invalids' Walk, one of the many walks through the pines.

Naturally there were ordinary pools and ponds in several places. There was one where Came built the Royal but I guess it must have drained all right as the foundations were solid. Mind you, he did do some daft things, like putting cellars in houses built on land which always flooded after a bit of rain.'

Woodhall did very well from the accidental discovery of spa water but after World War I the Baths were in financial trouble. Visiting a spa wasn't so fashionable and others, like Buxton, were suffering too. Also there were more people with motorcars who could visit a place for a day, rather than staying there. But people in Woodhall blamed the fact that the Victoria had burned down for the losses of the Baths. They thought visitors didn't want to stay anywhere else.

In fact, there were still hopes of rebuilding the hotel in 1925, five years after the fire. Sir Archibald Weigall bailed out the Baths when he returned from Australia in 1922 but he couldn't go on paying out indefinitely. Major Hotchkin said something must be done, that all the trades people would suffer and Woodhall Spa would die if the Baths went. There were village meetings about it and just about every family was represented. The Baths needed £500 a year to keep running and the problem was everybody was afraid of an increase in the rates if the U.D.C. took over the losses.

Actually, the U.D.C. couldn't legally do this, so Major Hotchkin and Sir Archibald Weigall went to London to meet the Minister of Health about it and obtained permission. There were still mutterings about the situation and enquiries as to who had authorised this trip to London and later, a Ratepayers Association was formed.

'Yes, I don't think they were fair to Sir Archibald about this. I heard he'd paid out over £1000. They said he got permission for the council to take the Baths over by calling them 'Public Wash-houses'!

He did quite a lot for Woodhall by knowing how to go about things, who to talk to. They said that Coningsby aerodrome was planned to be on Kirkby Lane – planes used to take off on grass in those days. But Weigall and other powers that be wouldn't hear of it – noise and everything – and it didn't happen.

When I finished school, at the end of the Twenties, I worked in the nursery, which stretched up from the station to the Methodist Chapel – Spa Road now. The present chapel was, in fact, the original, before a new one, now Fordman Computers, was built. There used to be a lovely willow pond at the top of Spa Road but the willows have all gone now. Yes, times change. My father talked of how potatoes were packed in boxes and sent off by train, in the old days. They found there was so much pilfering that, in the end, they padlocked the boxes and posted the key! We were still old-fashioned in many ways – we had our own well for water and kept pigs for manure.

The busy and important time for flowers each year was the lily season – lilies of the valley which grew profusely all around here. In fact, this area was good for wild flowers in general. At one time, before a couple of fires and the development of it as it is now, Ostlers Plantation was supposed to have one of the largest collections of wild flowers in the country. The lily harvest was from about the middle of May when there were many visitors here. The flowers were packed into boxes of one, two or three bunches to be sent all over the country. There were bunches for sale outside the dairy on the Broadway every summer. Our lilies were from Scrivelsby, from a wood of oak trees belonging to the King's Champion. They grew very well under the oaks and were always a fortnight earlier than anywhere else. They were estate picked and we packed them up at the Marmion pub at Haltham. On a good day we might have one hundred and twenty bunches.

It had been a tradition that the Dymokes always sent the first bunch picked, each year, to Queen Alexandra. In the end the oaks were felled – a high price was being paid for the wood – so the lilies didn't grow so well.

Winter Gardens of the Royal Hotel.

Tattershall Road with the Royal Hotel on the right and Goodyears on the left.

Cottage Museum Collection.

The nursery stopped flowers in 1939 and concentrated on food – vegetables and lettuces, even sugar beet but that didn't help us, there just wasn't much profit to be made so we had to wind it down. The government was telling everyone to use their gardens for vegetables and the newspapers were full of advice about growing tomatoes and such like. I wasn't in the war, I don't know why, just wasn't called up. I had friends who were and who didn't come back. There was Bob Belton, whose father worked for Sleight and Crookes, the decorators and undertakers. My friend from schooldays, Peter Shaw, was killed in Belgium, in the first thrust. We were away from most of it, here in Woodhall but many people were injured and, I think, three were killed in August '43 when the parachute mines dropped on us. One landed in Dr. Armour's garden at Tasburgh Lodge and the other on Clarence Road, where the telephone exchange is now. That was quite near us and my mother was hurt. In fact, she never fully recovered. Hundreds of properties were damaged and the Royal Hotel was so bad it was going to cost too much to put right and they had to pull it down. Such a pity. During the war there were many Air Raid Wardens and the like, of course the black out had to be checked. Once I was told to put out my cigarette!

After the war I took over the greengrocery in Albany House. My grandfather had started it in 1901.

I really would have liked to work with horses. I did a lot of riding. Once, when I was quite young, I was riding back along Tattershall Road – no saddle or anything. Well, as I got into Woodhall Spa a steamroller let off steam and my horse got such a shock at the sudden 'whoosh' that it reared fearfully. I don't know how I managed to stay on!

Our greengrocery kept us busy. We used to supply hotels and restaurants – Petwood, Golf, Eagle and the Rodney and Magpies in Horncastle – as well as the housewives of Woodhall Spa. We stocked all the usual fruit and vegetables and anything which had come to be fashionable. We always needed a lot of melons and we had beautiful Italian peaches – the French ones weren't so good. The mornings were very busy with orders, early on. It was all right when the railway was here because we got our stuff from Covent Garden and as long as we 'phoned our order through by 7.30am it was here, at the station at 1.00pm. After the railway closed we had to deal with wholesalers. I remember the first scales we had without weights. They cost about £60 but we were told they would pay for themselves. The pointer rounded up the weight but that made very little difference to greengrocery prices!

My wife and I worked hard in the business and we knew all the customers – at first anyway. The village has grown out of all recognition. It was nice to feel we were helping people as well as running a business. Some of the older folk were a bit confused when decimal currency came in and we've often been asked for advice – even how much someone should pay for a suit, on one occasion!

Sadly, my wife died in 1990, just before our Silver Wedding, but here I am living just round the corner from where I was born.'

There he is indeed, still interested in this place, past and present, still full of anecdotes and reminiscences, still busy in his garden, a lively gentleman with a charming smile, still to be seen, around <u>his</u> village.

FULLY LICENSED.   OWN GROUNDS.
GARAGE.   LIVERY STABLES.
Open throughout the Year.   Tariff on application to Miss LAMB.

Telegrams:
"EAGLE, WOODHALL SPA."
×
Telephone **32.**

Eagle Lodge Hotel.

Spa Hotel.

Recorded recollections of Frank Goodyear
of the family of butchers in Woodhall Spa

'My family opened a butchery business in Witham Road, in about 1890, when we came here from Haltham – incidentally, that used to be pronounced 'Halltam.' We moved round the corner to Tattershall Road in about 1911. We faced the Royal Hotel and adjoined the railway.

When I left school I worked in the family business. My brother, Jack, was in the Royal Flying Corps for the war and then became a Fleet Air Arm pilot and worked in civil aviation.

In my early days Woodhall Spa was a different place in the Season. As I recall, several houses were only occupied then. Society used to walk out after dinner and strut up and down around the Bandstand. They used to have four meals a day at the Victoria and at dinner there'd be seven or eight courses. I think it cost twelve shillings and sixpence a day (62½p in money of today) to stay there. When it went up in flames people dumped furniture on the lawn. The fire bell was near The Mall, with steps like a ladder to reach it to give the alarm. But the Victoria hadn't a chance, it was hopeless and then someone noticed that the wine cellars were full, so . . . That was not a normal Easter day.

Geoffrey Espin Esq.

Geoffrey, now in Heatherlea Residential Care Home, worked as a kitchen porter at The Golf Hotel for over twenty years towards the end of the twentieth century.

He remembers stars such as Magnus Magnusson, David Attenborough and some of the cast of Coronation Street visiting the hotel, as well as well-known golfers. He particularly remembers the celebration for the Queen's Silver Jubilee, in 1977, when six hundred and fifty people were served, in addition to the ninety golfers who were staying at the hotel.

There were several changes of ownership and various managers during his time. He recalls Mr. Fothergill coming into the kitchen and saying to the chef 'I'd put that pudding by the back door, it'll do as a doorstop.' On another occasion he asked the hapless cook, 'Have you ever thought of working in the crem.?'

The Golf Hotel (formerly the Clevedon Hotel).

Cottage Museum Collection.

St Hughs.

Cottage Museum Collection.

Mr. and Mrs. Forbes, founders, with Sheila and Fiona at the time of their Silver Wedding 1950.

H. D. Martineau

CHAPTER IV

Recorded reflections of Mrs. Ida Raw
wife of Sergeant Raw, early teacher at St. Hugh's School

"I was a Woodhall girl. My mother, Annie Sneath, had Claremont boarding house. We owned it for fifty years. Visitors in the Season usually came for three weeks treatment. Sometimes they brought maids and they were given rooms at the top of the house. Often every room was taken.

I remember when the parachute mines dropped, during the war. Claremont was quite near. It was in the middle of the night and we had to get everybody up! It wasn't easy and one visitor, in particular, was awfully deaf! It was a shame about the Royal Hotel. The brickwork was all right but glass was everywhere and the frames were useless.

But that wasn't so terrible for the village as the end of the Victoria Hotel, twenty-three years earlier. They said that the night porter was asleep, at first, that night, so the fire had time to take hold. It had been raining all day so there was a lot of linen airing which caught fire, and then the Lincoln fire engine broke down on the way here. In any case, the nearest water was on the Broadway so the fire had time to spread from end to end. Someone said it was like pouring water from a kettle.

I used to go by train to Horncastle Grammar School. Often we saw Johnny Wield with a bath chair. Sometimes he pushed one himself but it was usually pulled by a donkey and he would chat to the lady in the chair. He was a very particular man and he did everything for his wife, Asenath.

I was in the pageant in 1911. I was eighteen and it all seemed very romantic, out of doors and with beautiful costumes. The Weigalls were important in it. He was Hereward the Wake and she was very imposing as Hereward's wife, Torfrida.

When Lady Weigall first came to Woodhall, to the Baths, she was still married to that German Baron and she had a detective with her. When she married Captain Weigall there were cheering crowds when they came back from their honeymoon. The carriage was pulled by men and she threw out pennies and sweets. She loved it, you could see, and so did we!

I married Sergeant Raw, who was an army man, of course. Probably because of that he was a very disciplined man with a strong sense of duty as well as being very fit and strong. He started at St. Hugh's Preparatory School in 1930 and he was there for thirty-eight years. He taught games and swimming and boxing and woodwork and helped generally. When the school moved to Ingleton, all in a rush, he personally carried all the boys trunks across the platform and onto the train! He was very popular, I think, and he was certainly very busy – I hardly ever saw him!

Sergeant Raw loved St. Hugh's. He was never the same after he finished there."

Recorded reminiscences of Mrs. Joan Forbes
wife of the first Headmaster of St. Hugh's Preparatory School for Boys, Woodhall Spa

"My father was a golfer who had helped to design the golf course at Torksey, near Lincoln. Major S. V. Hotchkin, owner of the golf course at Woodhall Spa, sometimes asked his advice and so we knew the village well.

"Dominies", Headmaster's house, formerly Austral House, bought in 1952.

H. D. Martineau.

1926 – First pupils, standing: Montgomery, Wall; middle: Steele, Mr. Forbes, Dick Bellwood; front: Bob Bellwood, Hoare.

Cromwell Avenue, after first extensions.

St. Hugh's School.

Boating Pool at Fairmead (Spiller and Jakeman).

H. D. Martineau.

My husband and I were teachers and we saw the need for a boys school here, so in September 1925, we rented the large house on the corner of Iddesleigh Road and Stanhope Avenue. We started with just one pupil! Next term there were six and from then on it seemed to be all activity – appointing staff and domestics, renting the house next door and then the field to use for football and cricket. After a while we bought the house and field on Cromwell Avenue, which became the nucleus of the present school. There always seemed to be buying and building. We built the dining room and dormitories, the main block of classrooms and, later again, the carpenter's shop. We involved the boys whenever we could. They started digging a swimming pool from the rock garden and when we made a rugger pitch from the bottom field, the boys each planted a poplar and took care of it, to make a wind break. Each boy had a garden plot to look after as well. The woods grew right up to the school then and an artesian well of spa water was carefully guarded.

We thought we'd be all right here when war was declared but the army wanted the school building, so we had to go. We found Storrs Hall at Ingleton, in Yorkshire, which had once been a school and moved there, all in one week! The boys soon settled there and, as well as the ordinary curriculum, they learned to knit scarves for the war effort and filled many sandbags! After the war there would have been a refugee centre in St. Hugh's if we hadn't come back. The building was undamaged but the field had been used as an assault course and was a bit of a mess!

After the war the school really grew and a lot of juniors came in. At first many people, particularly Poles who were here during the war, helped with gardens etc. until new staff were demobilised. Then the school went from strength to strength in numbers and scholastic and sporting achievement. We bought further neighbouring properties and soon we were building again!"

Richard Bellwood Esq.
early pupil at St. Hugh's

"I was born in the Manor House, South Carlton, near Lincoln, where my father farmed. That was in 1915. My mother was a vicar's daughter, who was brought up in London and, by coincidence, went to the same school as Neil Hotchkin's mother.

For a short while I went to school on Wragby Road, Lincoln, and then my mother heard about St. Hugh's and, in 1926, when I was ten and a bit, I was sent here with my brother Robert, who was eighteen months younger. The school was on the corner of Iddesleigh Road and Stanhope Avenue then. It had opened the previous term with Ray Hoare, from Reeds Beck, as the only pupil! There were just a handful of us at first so it was more like a family than a school, particularly as Mr. and Mrs. Forbes were quite young. He was from Portadown, Northern Ireland and had a strong Ulster accent. Mrs. Forbes' father was another vicar, the Reverend Watney, at Canwick, Lincoln. The Forbes had been teaching in Sussex but they had married at Canwick and found this property for a school here.

Anyway, I remember being put on a train and we were met at the station, at Kirkstead by Mr. Forbes and taken to the school. We soon settled into a routine. The day was from about 8 until 8, as I remember and I seemed to be taught English, Maths., History and Geography, mostly. Then Mr. Forbes started woodwork with his father-in-law, which Sergeant Raw took over when he arrived after I'd been at school three or four years. Sergeant Raw was a disciplinarian and our physical training exercises were like army drill! I still have two little wooden boxes, one with an owl embossed on top, which I made with him. I don't remember being taught Science but Nature Study we learnt when we were outside. We used to go to St. Andrew's church on Sunday mornings and, on fine Sunday afternoons, Mrs. Forbes would take us out in the car for a picnic and she'd talk a bit about trees and flowers we saw.

On other afternoons we had games. Rugby hadn't started then but we played football. Of course, for a while there weren't enought of us for proper teams. The playing field was behind the school, where houses have been built now, along Iddesleigh Road.

When we were in the village we had to wear the school cap and raise it to people we passed. The story of the badge on the cap is interesting. It shows a ball above a wall and is from the story of a boy who was murdered when fetching his ball from over the Jew's house in Lincoln. I think the point was that we should always be in control of what we are doing and only be where permitted!

I went to Oakham School after St. Hugh's. My brother passed a scholarship to Worksop and then went on to Cambridge.

In 1934, I joined the Royal Marines and served on "HMS Queen Elizabeth," the flagship of the Mediterranean fleet. I was on "HMS Rodney" when war was declared and we had to go into port to have the ship's bottom scraped and be made ready for action. Later, I served on the "Prince of Wales". We were often in danger, of course, but it was when we were outside Singapore we were torpedoed by the Japanese. There were 1,500 on board and even though we knew all about emergency measures, there was very little time with so many people and many of us died. Those of us who survived were floating on the water and picked up by "HMS Express." It was a chilling experience to watch the "Prince of Wales" go down.

At the end of the war, my parents were living in the Manor House, Kirkstead. My father was poultry farming – all free range in those days – and I helped for a while before starting poultry on my own between the golf course and Sandy Lane. So, here I am still, in this village I came to as a lad, over three quarters of a century ago."

Roy Cox Esq.
teacher at St. Hugh's and later Deputy Head of Gartree Secondary School

"My parents and I came to Woodhall Spa in 1947 and lived on the top floor of Claremont House on Witham Road, where my mother was cook and my father gardener. He had been a farm worker at Greetham where I went to school, before passing the Scholarship Examination for Horncastle Grammar School.

In 1949 I wanted to join the RAF but was pronounced unfit because I had acne! So I had a variety of temporary jobs – for the Council, the Post Office, the Water Board – until, in 1950, Mr. Taylor, Head of Horncastle Grammar School, recommended me to Mr. Forbes for a teaching post in French at St. Hugh's. Well, I had Higher School Certificate French but Geography was my subject and I had no teaching experience at all! Anyhow, I went to see Mr. Forbes but some parents arrived to see him, so an appointment was made for a few days later – when the same thing happened! Eventually, on the first day of term, a timetable was thrust into my hand and I was shown my classroom! I was only at the school for a couple of years but I have vivid and happy memories.

There were 144 boys there, 75% of whom were local." N.B. a photograph of 1950 has a small cross legged Bob Fletcher, farmer and Golf Club Past Captain, gazing cherubically at the camera. "The day began at 7.45am. There were prayers and breakfast and the children all had to go to the bathroom before lessons. We had a plywood board with their names and they were ticked off as they returned! Lessons began at 9 o'clock and they were expected to work hard – success in Common Entrance, at 13, was necessary for the school's reputation. Discipline was important from the start. Most children came from good homes but self discipline was expected at school and etiquette, manners and politeness were important. The boys raised their caps to people in the street and good behaviour was expected outside as well as inside school. Games were played every afternoon. In winter Rugby was the first game and, after teams were chosen, the others played Soccer. In summer they were well coached in cricket and there was swimming. Mr. Martineau started rifle shooting with them when he joined the staff. In an evening there was Prep. and the boys had some time to themselves when tuck boxes and toys were brought out and shared – they were good at sharing.

I found some things irksome. Obviously the school had to be a paying proposition but sometimes economy seemed to be taken too far! For example, marking was done with a red pencil (this was before the time of biros) and when it became too small to sharpen we had to take it to the stockroom to prove a new one was necessary. When exam. time came the masters bought trays of jelly from Mortons, the printers on Broadway. The jelly was boiled and spread in the trays. A special pen and mauve ink were used to write out the exam. paper, which was pressed onto the jelly and peeled off. Further papers were pressed on until the ink became too smeared. This was a form of duplicating far removed from later photocopying.

Many teachers stayed at St. Hugh's for years and several, such as Bunny and John Game, still live in Woodhall Spa.

By 1951 my acne had disappeared but the services were no longer recruiting! I decided to go to college for a teaching qualification, which would also help financially. At St. Hugh's I had board and lodging and was paid £50 a term. Of course, I was only 19 and unqualified. After qualifying in 1953 I was earning £24 17s 2d a month – but the 2d was still very important!"

Mrs. Jean Barr teacher at St. Hugh's and her husband, Allen, who became Deputy Head

In 1951 Miss Jean Pickup joined the staff of St. Hugh's, to teach general subjects to the juniors. A Lancashire lass from Rochdale, she had trained at Westfield College, London, with Mary Stocks as Principal. Having applied for the post here, she was invited by Mr. Forbes to come and look round. She was astonished upon arrival, to realise that she had come across boys from St. Hugh's before. As a small girl on holiday at Ingleton, Yorkshire, in 1940, she had seen them walking up from the station to Storrs Hall. "It was the badge on the distinctive red caps that I recognised," says Jean. "The pavement was a couple of feet below our garden and I remember flicking out pebbles with my feet as they passed!"

Knowing that Maths. was her subject, after Jean had been at the school a little while, Mr. Forbes asked her to listen to him taking a class in the subject. Then she had to repeat the lesson to the children in the next room. This she successfully accomplished and so became an addition to the Maths. Department. "Yes, the idea of a woman teaching Maths. in a boys Prep. School was unheard of," reflects Jean.

Two years after her appointment, Allen Barr came as a Geography master and to coach Rugby. "I soon settled in at the school" says Allen "the atmosphere was friendly and, if your face fitted, by which I mean if you were prepared to work and take a real interest, Mr. Forbes was very fair."

Jean and Allen became friendly, although one might imagine that a romance in residential school surroundings would not be easy. "Oh but the senior boys were wonderful. Allen and

"Drill" on the lawn.

H. D. Martineau

Scene from A. A. Milne's play
"Make Believe" 1936.
(left to right: H. Spurrier,
P. Gurnhill, A. Davis, H. Foster,
M. Goodworth, H. Strawson,
H. Larr, D. Harrison,
R. Dixon, C. R. Grantham,
M. Pennington).

St. Hugh's boys knitting comforts in World War II, the first boy on the front row left is
Norman Wright (later Chairman of Governors, now deceased).

St. Hugh's School.

I would go for a walk in the evening after our duties and they would say "Go on Miss Pickup, he's waiting for you, we'll finish the clearing up."

I lived at Glenesk, on Broadway, with other ladies. The atmosphere was quite Victorian and I had to be in by 10 o'clock at night. I was 21 at the time! The men were treated differently in other ways too – no supper was prepared for us ladies and, of course, we were not paid the same salary. In those days salaries were very small. We were paid at the end of each half term and term, so at the end of July we had all the summer holidays and weren't paid again until the middle of October. It was difficult to manage when our children were small.

One of the characters I remember was Miss Dennison. She had played the violin with the London Philharmonic Orchestra. She was a very independent lady. She was at the school for 15 years, I think but to everyone was always, "Miss Dennison."

"Another was Jack Fletcher," reflects Allen. "He was the gardener and groundsman but he was also a gravedigger so if there was a funeral he'd be off to that, which didn't always please Mr. Forbes! He was popular with the boys though and they would give him money to buy sweets for them.

But Mr. and Mrs. Forbes were the real characters. Mrs. Forbes was rather straight-laced and could be a formidable lady, very strong. Mr. Forbes was an enthusiast. He worked very hard himself and expected others to do the same. He was generous and kind but also firm and, obviously, had business acumen. He also had a sense of humour and liked to make the punishment fit the crime." The story is related in Hugh Martineau's book, "Half a Century of St. Hugh's," of a boy who side stepped from the line filing into assembly, in order to read a comic in the cloakroom. He was discovered and Mr. Forbes presented him with a bedside pot and sympathising with his weak bladder, suggested he carried it everywhere and put it on the halfway line during Games that day!

"Mr. Forbes would turn his hand to anything, which needed doing. The story was told of how once he was casually dressed, striding down the rugby field, carrying swill to the pigs in the swampy bit at the bottom, when he was approached by prospective parents who asked where they could find the headmaster! He would charm them. He was good with parents and could always reassure anxious mums. He personally read every report we wrote and there were 180 pupils when I started at the school. There were places for general comments, such as weight and height, on the report, as well as scholastic results. One, of a new boy, reputedly read, "Height, beginning of term, 4' 2", end of term, 4' 1½"." Headmaster's comment, "Johnny seems to be settling down nicely." He was a kind man and would sometimes waive fees or charge less if parents were going through hard times." "I remember him being very nice to me on one occasion," remarks Jean. "I used to take country dancing and one of the boys was so naughty that I really lost my temper. I regretted it straight away and told Mr. Forbes. "Try not to worry," he said, kindly, "When you are married you'll find that sometimes your temper has to match theirs." "I've often thought of this since – Allen and I have 4 children! Mr. Forbes would do anything for his family and his school, which became his family. His daughters did very well. Sheila went to Oxford and became an engineer, which was very unusual for girls in the Fifties. Fiona went to Cambridge before a successful career."

Allen continues, "Boys were given the cane or slipper as punishment, sometimes, in those early days, but not often. There was a system of black marks and golds but, in the seventies, extra work or detention took the place of blacks.

The boys were well looked after and well fed. On Thursdays, sausages and kidneys came from Ireland and, on Fridays, whole cod were bought from Grimsby. On Saturdays there were joints of beef.

There were various trips and visits and we took the boys to ski in Norway. On the first occasion, in 1956, we were approached by a Norwegian in Bergen, who recognised the school cap! Apparently he had been to Skegness.

Mr. Forbes died in 1960, after which the format of the school changed. A council of 12 governors, chaired by the Bishop of Lincoln was formed in 1961 and this became a charitable trust three years later. Mrs. Forbes continued for a while after her husband's death, before the short stay of a new head, Mr. Vincent and then Mr. Michael Wheeler.

From then there was much development, particularly physically, in the school buildings. "I was teaching Maths. and Geography and I started the new Science Lab. until Steve Langley came as Science Master," explains Allen. "I was appointed Deputy Head in Mr. Wheeler's time. He was a clear seeing head and with the support of the governors, he got things done. He was head hunted by Cheam School and left after 10 years at St. Hugh's."

Mr. Michael Kelham became Head in 1972 and the new building continued with many successful money raising events and dinners, gifts from old pupils and covenants for tax benefits. The new Assembly Hall, with a stage for plays and concerts, was named Forbes Hall and opened by Mrs. Thatcher. "Yes, she had been Minister for Education when she agreed to come but by the time it happened she was leader of the Conservative Party," comments Jean, "but she still came and Airey Neave and her press secretary, Bernard Ingham, were with her. She knew Woodhall Spa from her Grantham days. She was charming and very natural – she said she had brought hats with her in the back of the car, in case she needed them. I was astonished at the amount of security for her visit. Detectives even examined the pot plants in the hall."

Girls were admitted to the school in the 1980s. "Sometimes, girly things were difficult to fit in but I taught them sewing," Jean reflects. "Yes, but what they really wanted was to play rugger," says Allen. "They'd watched the boys and begged me to let them play. In the end I agreed and I had a real shock. They really set to with flying tackles – I thought they were going to kill each other! I had to stop it quickly – they hadn't had any training and I could have been in real trouble if there'd been an accident.

School life wasn't all lessons and games. Saturday night was cinema night, when John Game showed a film. The Dambusters was popular at Christmas, I remember."

"Oh, and Sports Days were memorable occasions," adds Jean. "They were in May or June and everyone was dressed up – Woodhall's answer to Ascot! There was a marquee for visitor's teas and the boys would go in and finish off the food afterwards!

The school did pretty well, scholastically and the boys went on to most of the public schools. The Clark brothers from Grimsby or Cleethorpes were at Gordonstoun at the same time as Prince Andrew. Many of our pupils were fairly local but we had some from far-flung places. There was even a Danish prince and a Nigerian family of eight children – well there were four, different, colourfully robed, mothers. Their father had a flour factory in USA and he used to pay the bills in dollars – cash! Some pupils were from wealthy families but they all mixed well in school. I remember one boy talking, in a matter of fact way, about his family's racehorses. "Well," said another, "but I've got a donkey."

"There was a 'do' at Petwood, when I retired in 1993," Allen continues, "120 boys from the '50s to '90s were there. They filed past and I was able to remember all their names – well, they were rugger players coming to see Paddy leave the pitch!" "Living here we still feel in touch with the school which was very much part of our lives for 40 years."

David Radford Esq.
teacher at St. Hugh's and Deputy Head for some years, before his retirement in July 2002

"It does seem only yesterday that I found my way to Lincolnshire, Woodhall Spa and St. Hugh's School – all very much unknown quantities to a Cardiffian like myself but providing an opportunity to teach Latin in a well established preparatory school, so worth taking the risk!

Mr. Wheeler, the then Headmaster, was waiting to meet me at Grantham Station and I soon found myself captivated by his description of the school. This together with the beauty of the Spa's tree-lined avenues gently persuaded me into a relationship with the school and Spa, which has provided a home for my family for some thirty-four years!

St. Hugh's is a school which moves with the times and those years have incorporated a number of changes which I feel would have met with the approval of the first headmaster Mr. Ronald (Ronnie) Forbes and his wife, Joan.

In 1969 when I took charge of the Latin department there were only boys at the school; well it was officially known as a boys' independent boarding school but there was a 'smattering' of girls – daughters of staff and a few friends of the school from the local community.

The boys of '69 wore short grey cords, even 'the giants' of sixth form, until they left for public school and pastures new! They were expected to wear their school uniform, blazers, mackintoshes and caps on their 'crocodile' route to Church every Sunday morning. Whilst the red blazer still features as part of the smart, modern wardrobe of both boys and girls, the mackintoshes (macs and caps) have disappeared from the lists!

These boys would mostly have had their hair cut by the local barber – Jack Hyde was his name. This was a moment to dread, some might say, but Jack was no demon and ran a successful business until his retirement many years later with a regular supply of St. Hugh's pupils. Nowadays the boys and girls visit their own favourite hairdresser! There has been no change to the compliments the pupils receive when on their various trips to the theatre, museums and sporting engagements. Needless to say, a source of great pride to the school.

The arrival of the girls in 1980 was a momentous occurrence in the school's history although, dare I say it, some parents did not approve of the co-educational principle! However, these reactions soon disappeared after that first year and the brothers and sisters and cousins who arrived have made St. Hugh's a family school with a wonderful atmosphere often noted by visitors. I well remember a chance remark once made to me, "I can feel the happiness in the walls," which I found quite fascinating as this was made by a visitor on a first visit to the school, empty of pupils during the school holidays!!

It is a real pleasure to see those who have known St. Hugh's many years ago return to refresh their memories of those early days in their education. Whilst there are the same familiar places, the dining hall and dormitories figuring high on their list, they are surprised and impressed by the development of the school's facilities, which have taken place over the years, facilities that are often shared with the local village, expecially the Sports Hall, the swimming pool and the Forbes Hall. The opening of the Forbes Hall by the Rt. Hon. Mrs. Margaret Thatcher and later on that of the Norman Wright Sports Hall by HRH the Duchess of Gloucester were never to be forgotten occasions as was the opening of the Kelham Centre by the Bishop of Lincoln. These, together with the classroom block and library, the Pre-Prep and Nursery and, of course, the dedication of the teachers and the

Mr. Allen Barr with class in science laboratory.

Mr. Michael Wheeler, M.A.
Headmaster 1962-72.

Mr. Michael Kelham, M.A.
Headmaster 1972-1994.

Building of eight new classrooms in 1972 and Assembly Hall
completed in 1974.

H. D. Martineau

vivacity of the pupils, all combine to show the present day strengths of the school they once knew and a school still known in the 21st century as Lincolnshire's Premier Preparatory School.

Thoughts of Michael Kelham, Esq.
Headmaster of St. Hugh's from 1972-1994.

"Marian and I arrived at St. Hugh's in April 1972 when the school was emerging from the difficulties it had experienced after the death of Ronnie Forbes. Its reputation was running high particularly among the Lincolnshire farming community, thanks largely to the efforts of my predecessor, Michael Wheeler.

Coming to Woodhall was for me almost like a homecoming. I was born in Lincolnshire, as were my parents and my grandfather, Walter Kelham, retired to the village in about 1949. He lived in "Derwent" in Iddesleigh Road and his long, narrow garden stretched to the corner of "Dominies," the Headmaster's house – a small world!

One of my concerns working in a rural boarding school was that the job could be all consuming and very introspective. During term time it is possible to be totally absorbed in school life from early in the morning until late at night. I tried therefore to encourage members of staff to develop outside interests and to become involved in some aspect of village life. I myself played cricket, hockey and tennis for the village teams and for a while held the unlikely office of Chairman of the Chamber of Trade. In later years I became a member of the newly formed Rotary Club.

Similarly, I felt that the pupils needed their horizons extending beyond the school boundaries. The building of the Forbes Hall enabled us to expand our programme of inviting visiting speakers and performers to come and share their experiences with the pupils, parents and staff. Thus was born the "Arts Club," so ably run by David Radford for many years. We succeeded in attracting men and women of international repute to the school and their lectures and recitals did much to enrich the education of the children. They also provided an opportunity for parents and staff to mingle in a relaxed and friendly atmosphere, which is an important aspect of prep school life.

Another venture, which strengthened the ties between parents and staff, was the formation, in 1973, of the Parents' Association. Members of the committee worked very hard to organise many highly successful social functions, which not only brought people together informally, but also raised considerable sums of cash to benefit the pupils at the school.

The social life of the school is very important but it has to take second place to the school's primary function – to provide as good an education as possible for the pupils. Children will only produce their best if the atmosphere is warm and comfortable and everyone at St. Hugh's worked hard to achieve the fine balance between an over-strict discipline and one that is too relaxed. From my first day I called the boys (yes, they were all boys in those days!) by their Christian names and I abolished the use of the cane. At the same time I stressed the need for good manners, courtesy and thought for others – themes pursued regularly in our daily act of worship. I like to think that we struck the right balance most of the time for most of the pupils.

This 'softening' of the atmosphere helped considerably in the transition to co-education, which took place in 1980 when the school was fortunate enough to buy Raftsund, the house belonging to former pupil Henry Foster and his mother. The purchase of the house and its lovely garden gave us much more space and the advent of girls inevitably brought changes. Boys for instance, no longer had to play the part of females in the annual school play and the musical side of school life in particular was greatly enhanced by their presence in the choir and orchestra.

I am often asked if I miss the life; of course I do. What I miss most are the highlights of the school year – the Carol Service in St. Peter's, the school play, usually a musical, and Sports Weekend, when we used to hold our inter-house athletics on the Saturday followed by pupils v. parents at all manner of games on the Sunday. I think it is very sad that this occasion no longer exists. It used to promote and advertise all that was best about St. Hugh's, but no doubt other things have taken its place.

What I don't miss are the long hours spent writing reports, preparing assemblies and sorting out problems! But they were all part of the job and running a good prep school is a marvellous job; I have no regrets.

During our 22 years in Woodhall we had some wonderful times, met some fascinating people and made some very good friends. I hope we also provided a stimulating and friendly environment for those who worked at the school and for the many hundreds of boys and girls who spent what were perhaps the most formative years of their lives under its roof.

The appointment of the head of a boarding prep school is almost always a joint husband and wife appointment and I cannot leave this brief account without expressing my appreciation for the support offered by Marian, who was not only involved in overseeing various domestic aspects of school life but who also had to cope with bringing up our own children, Tim, Adrian and Chris. Life was not always easy for her nor for the boys being educated in their father's school as this was bound to put pressures on them. Fortunately, I think they have all survived!

Woodhall is a unique place and I shall always treasure my memories of it. As my mother is still alive and living in Eastwood Lodge, I have every excuse to come and visit! But she will be 103 shortly so these visits may not last much longer and I shall be the sadder for that."

The Broadway, Woodhall Spa.

A postcard sent by "Elephantina", in 1905.

CHAPTER V

Recorded information from
Mrs. Renee Ismanycka, née Collins

"My father came to work for Carlton, the chemist, in 1901. Horncastle Road was just a sandy lane between gorse bushes then. My brothers and I used to cycle up it following the hounds.

I went to Miss Lunn's school in Hartington House. The Misses Lunn were rather peculiar and not business-like. I once saw Miss Susannah listening at the keyhole of a noisy classroom to catch out the teacher! I remember a stove with a big iron fender round it and once, after Bonfire Night, we girls collected used fireworks and threw them on the fire. Well, one, a Jumping Jack, wasn't dead and it went off! Miss Cupples, who was teaching us, had a dreadful fright and jumped about in an awful state. Once, Lady Weigall invited Miss Lunn's girls to Petwood and showed us round. We were impressed with the lavishness of everything and there was a large cupboard absolutely full of her shoes. The Weigalls called at the shop and gave us Christmas presents. In 1918, at the end of the war, Captain Weigall rode to church on a horse for the thanksgiving service.

It was fun to see visitors in the Season. The men wore cream flannels, striped blazers and straw hats and ladies had expensive dresses. One lady walked out with a cat on her shoulder and another carried a parrot on the spokes of her sunshade. It bit my father's finger!

The Baths were at the centre of it all but there was sometimes trouble there. Mr. Lewis was an awkward man. He once stopped my mother from going across the railway crossing and past the Baths to Petwood. She was a Red Cross Nurse and was going to join a British Legion Parade. So she had to go all the way round, past the shops and along Stixwould Road. Afterwards, Sir Archibald said that if he'd known he'd have marched the whole legion through! In the end Sir Archibald took the Baths over again. Colonel Hotchkin organised it, I think. Sir Archibald wouldn't have any dealings with Mr. Lewis!

I remember the Fango treatment at the Baths. The patient lay on a table with hot towels. There was a door at the side of the room and mud was brought up from the cleaning of the adits of the well. It was thought that the mud would contain all the minerals of the water. So warm mud was applied and then the patient was wrapped in hot towels. Of course, we all thought the treatments were very beneficial. I'm sure I once saw a lady arrive for the Season in a spinal carriage who could jump over a gate before she left!

Dr. George Armour
from an account by his son, Dr. A. J. ("Sandy") Armour

"My father arrived in Woodhall Spa in the late 1920s with £16 and a bicycle. He came to work as an assistant in General Practice to Dr. Leonard Boys. Previously he had been employed by Dr. Boys' father, in St. Albans, as a trainee, on a salary of £52 per annum, all found! Dr.Leonard Boys described himself as a Spa Physician, working from the Baths and the Alexandra Hospital (now "The Alexandra"). He lived at the Dower House where he had a consulting room. When my father arrived, the Tasburgh Lodge Practice had been constantly changing hands, so there were only 23 patients on the panel! Dr. Boys told my father that he did not do night visits or midwifery or attend children, all of which were important aspects of General Practice.

Carlton & Sons,
Chemists shop.

D. N. Robinson

Workers with heavy
equipment at the Baths.

Cottage Museum Collection.

The original Spa Bath
house built by Thomas
Hotchkin in the 1830s.

My father was given a salary of £500 per annum, a motorcar, Tasburgh Lodge as a service tenancy, a maid, a gardener and a "car boy." Tasburgh Lodge was a large Edwardian house, built by a Dr. Gwyn who came from the village of Tasburgh, in Norfolk, hence the name. It was purpose built as a doctor's house. Private patients came through the front door and waited in their own waiting room, which was furnished with armchairs! They came by appointment. Panel patients (employed persons registered under the Lloyd George 1921 Act) came in by a separate side entrance at the servants end of the house and sat on leather-covered benches. They were seen in a sparser consulting room in order of their arrival – the old "sit and shuffle" method, so called to describe the way they moved up the bench. Between the private and panel suites was the dispensary where all medicines, mostly liquid in 4, 8, 10 or 12 fluid ounce bottles, were mixed, bottled and labelled.

As the Practice expanded my father opened a branch practice at Bucknall and, after a while, he was appointed Assistant Physician at the Spa Baths and Alexandra Hospital and was also a member of staff at the hospital in Horncastle. There he performed operations such as appendicectomies, hernial repairs and even gall bladder removals! At this time, all babies, apart from Caesarean sections, were delivered at home. These included forceps deliveries, for which my father gave his own anaesthetics, usually chloroform.

To augment his income, my father was Medical Officer to the local London and North Eastern Railway, his remit extending in different directions to Louth, Retford and Peterborough. He supervised the fitness to work of all the employees and instructed the rail accident and emergency teams in First Aid, to a high standard. He was also an examiner in First Aid, at all levels, to other local voluntary organisations. In addition he was, for a time, Medical Officer of Health to the Urban District of Woodhall Spa. If one looks very carefully there may still be signs bearing his signature, for example at the beck down Kirkby Lane and also at the bridge over the same beck on Tattershall Road, "The water in this beck is not fit for human consumption."

By the Second World War the Woodhall Spa Baths had declined in popularity and the only place left for treatment was Mr. Fred Hardy's Clinic at "The Nook," on the corner of Iddesleigh Road and Broadway. Many of the larger homes were empty and these were requisitioned by the War Office and rapidly filled with soldiers. As a result Woodhall soon became a garrison town in which soldiers outnumbered civilians. My father was not called up, being retained to care for the local population and help Army and RAF doctors with their casualties. He also had to form, train and lead First Aid and Emergency teams in the area and be on special alert during air raid warnings. I well remember him going out with a "flying squad" to Kirkby on Bain when it was bombed and Bucknall when it had a near miss from an "aerial torpedo."

"My father was not at home on the night of 17th/18th August 1943, when Woodhall was bombed. Tasburgh Lodge was severely damaged and my mother badly hurt and hospitalised for the next four weeks. As the house was uninhabitable, my father, immediately, had to find somewhere for himself, my brother and myself to live, where he could continue his medical practice. After one or two temporary homes we moved into Stanhope House, Victoria Avenue and converted the two front rooms into consulting and waiting rooms, with the dispensary located in the housemaid's pantry! This move effectively ended patient discrimination!

However, by 1951 Tasburgh Lodge had been rebuilt, although to an entirely new design, rendering it very different from the surrounding Edwardian properties. As before it was purpose built, with a separate surgery wing. There was a private consulting room in the house itself with private patients entering by the front door and waiting in the family lounge! My father liked to be surrounded by his work.

With the end of the war in May and August 1945 the soldiers had rapidly left but were equally rapidly replaced by "Displaced Persons" from all over Europe, who took over the

Nissen huts and some of the requisitioned houses. Therefore my father was now confronted by Italian and German Prisoners of War waiting for repatriation and also Poles, Czechs, Ukrainians and Hungarians and others from former occupied countries. So now he had to cope with a language barrier, as there were few interpreters. I well remember children as young as three boldly interpreting for their mothers in the shops!

However, the big change came when Aneurin Bevan established the National Health Service in 1948. Everybody, including previous private patients, rapidly brought in their medical cards to register. It was a very busy time administratively but somehow my parents coped. Before the NHS, doctors worked on one third bad debts and very many unpaid bills remain so to this day!

Because most of Woodhall's inhabitants registered with my father he set up practice on his own and then was joined by Dr Robertson, three years later. This appointment was partly necessitated by my father having agreed to establish a centre for the treatment of Rheumatism and Allied Diseases for the whole of the Trent region, based at the Woodhall Spa Baths and Alexandra Hospital. In addition he was now doing outpatient sessions at Lincoln, Gainsborough, Sleaford and Boston hospitals and was one of the first doctors to hold outpatient sessions at the newly built Pilgrim Hospital, Boston, well before any wards were opened. In addition to this workload my father did domiciliary home visits throughout the county and often in South Yorkshire! Then, together with Dr. Lawy, Consultant Pathologist at Grimsby Hospital, he also carried out original research into a specific blood test for Rheumatoid Arthritis which was the forerunner of the current test for the Rheumatoid factor. After the results were presented to the Spa Federation (on the only occasion that the Annual General Meeting was held here) he was asked to read his paper all over Britain.

By the time I arrived in July 1959, as a Trainee Assistant, Dr. Robertson was also working at the Baths and Alexandra, finishing with the title of Hospital Practitioner in Rheumatology at Lincoln County Hospital, after the Baths finally closed to patients.

Meantime, in 1965, my father was summoned to Sheffield and, to his surprise, was offered the full-time post of Consultant Rheumatologist in the Sheffield region of the NHS.

After a wonderfully dedicated and varied career my father, eventually, reluctantly decided he must retire from the NHS because of increasing age. He was a lost soul doing locums when he received a telephone call from the Consultant in Rheumatology at the newly completed Queen's Medical Centre at Nottingham, asking him if he was available to conduct some outpatient and ward sessions there. This, plus work at the former very famous Harlow Wood Specialist Orthopaedic Hospital, near Mansfield, was salvation! After this he was able to phase out gradually into retirement.

The service pioneered by my father, initially alone and later with Dr. Robertson, now employs five, or possibly six, Consultant Rheumatologists in the county, with their entourages of junior medical staff as well as others serving South Yorkshire. Sadly, Woodhall Spa, once the centre, the mainspring of it all, can now only obtain these services from the main district hospital. Such is progress."

Dr. George Armour was one of the local people interviewed on the radio programme "Down Your Way" in 1976. He described the deep well at the Baths with hundreds of mollusc shells lining the walls of the shaft. He said he didn't prescribe drinking the water, a practice which was abandoned shortly after his arrival in the Spa but immersion baths, with physiotherapists in attendance, continued. The famous Spa water, rich in minerals and particularly bromine and iodine was more buoyant than ordinary water but some time before the Baths closed, that too was abandoned because of cost and technical difficulties. He felt the rehabilitation area at the Baths, where there was, for example, a kitchen in which severely crippled patients could relearn tasks such as turning taps and opening cans, was proving very beneficial.

Many people have a "Doctor George" anecdote. Mrs. Howsam says he "has a special place" with her because of his kindness when her husband was ill. Mr. Howsam suffered a series of small strokes and Dr. George told her she must call him "day or night" if she thought he'd had another.

Cecil Caudle recalled how, in about 1929, he broke his arm, which was set by a nearby vet. Next day he went to Dr. George who took him in his car to the Baths for an X-ray which Johnny Wield developed in about an hour. Luckily, the arm was pronounced "well set" and Cecil never did admit it had been done by a vet!

Ken Whyles describes how his father cut his finger very badly on a sprocket at the Kinema, whereupon Dr. George, in the audience, fixed it there and then.

Similarly, Joan Monk recalls an occasion in church when a member of the congregation suffered an epileptic fit and there was Dr. George striding up the aisle to cope. "He always seemed to be there when needed."

Dr. George Armour also had a reputation for being "straight" and calling a spade a spade. Joan Houldershaw remembers his scepticism about the latest "Diet Which Works." "Well," he said, "it may or may not but if you keep yourself hungry all the time you'll lose weight."

Mrs. Riley remembers taking her small son for a routine injection. Briskly, Dr. George instructed her "trousers down and put him across your knee." He then gave the boy a quick, light slap, followed by the injection and told the astonished lad, "That's what bottoms are for, slapping and injecting."

Finally, an anecdote from that well-known commentator, "Anon." Dr. George met a lady patient on the Broadway. He raised his hat politely, at which she stopped and said, "Oh doctor, I'm so glad to see you. I've an awful pain in my shoulder." "Oh dear," he replied, "well just slip your blouse off and I'll take a look at it."

Dr. James Robertson and the Healing Waters

James T. W. Robertson, M.D., M.B., Ch.B., 'Dr. Robertson' or 'Jim' as people know him, lives with his wife, Joan, in Victoria Avenue, Woodhall Spa. They came here in 1951 when he became a partner with the late Dr. George Armour, General Practitioner in the village.

Both he and his wife were a long way from home. Joan was brought up in Wales and Jim is a Scot, born in Edinburgh and educated at Glasgow High School before entering Glasgow University, to study Medicine, in 1939.

"Yes, I started at the University, just two or three weeks after World War II was declared," says Jim. "It was rather like still going to school in that I was there from 9 to 5 and then back with my family in the evening – not like student life as one thinks of it

Dr. James Robertson

today. There was a great deal of anxiety about the war and, of course, Glasgow and the shipyards of the Clyde were prime targets for the Germans. I was caught out in the open during saturation bombing of the city and docks in 1941."

It was in 1941 that the U.S.A. introduced the 'Rockefeller Scheme.' The war in Europe was going badly and the aim of the scheme was to have 'keepers of the flame' of British medicine, so that should there be a German invasion of the British Isles, our traditions and knowledge

The boiler room.

Barrel for lifting the water.

Cottage Museum Collection.

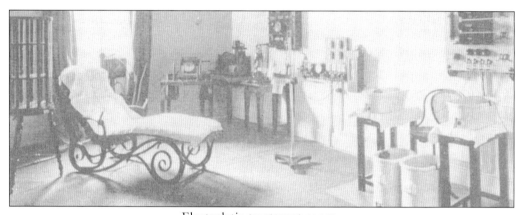

Electrolytic treatment room.

Woodhall Spa on old picture postcards.

Dowsing Radiant Heat Bath of eighty years ago.

The empty Rheumatology clinic, 1986. *Lincolnshire Life.*

would not be lost. This was to be achieved by Universities in America and Canada offering places to British students for the final two years of the course in medicine. As Jim points out this was long before the U.S. entered the war and at the country's own expense, funded by the Rockefeller Foundation. Between 1941 and 1944 there were 88 students selected. 45 were from Oxford, Cambridge and London, 25 from other English Universities and 18, Scots, Welsh and Irish. Five of these, of whom Jim was one, were from Glasgow University. It was an honour, indeed to be selected as one of this elite group.

So, in 1942, greatly excited but also, perhaps, very aware of leaving family in war-torn Glasgow and with a certain nervousness concerning the new venture, Jim set sail in a small British freighter, part of a 40 ship convoy. Life on the ocean wave must have been very different from in the heart of a large industrial city. Then, just over a fortnight after leaving port, on the night of August 2nd, the convoy was attacked by a pack of about five German U boats. Four ships, including the one in which Jim was sailing were holed and sank. One can imagine the sudden lights and flares, the shouted commands, the rushing movement, the feelings of uncertainty and panic. Jim and another student realised the ship was going down and there was confusion around the lifeboats (afterwards there was some enquiry as to the efficiency of the launching of the boats) so they decided to jump overboard and swim for it. Mercifully, they located a raft and were able to clamber onto it. Such rafts were called Carley Floats and were basically oil drums which had been bound together and encased. More and more survivors, too many, in fact, for safety, floundered to the raft and also one or two bodies bumped against them which the medical students assessed as dead but were unable to ascertain this definitely until later. It was very dark and silent. Suddenly, a large Canadian destroyer, searching for survivors, loomed alongside the raft. "We were very fortunate. He had no means of telling we were there," reflects Jim. "Ten of the passengers and crew died in the torpedo attack, one of whom was a Cambridge University medical student."

So, the survivors on the raft were picked up and spent 4 or 5 days at sea before docking at Halifax, Nova Scotia. There, Jim was kitted out with clothes etc. before boarding a train for Detroit and thence some 40 miles to Ann Arbor and the University of Michigan. Jim describes his two years there as "almost total delight," thoroughly enjoying the residential student life with its college songs and societies. He was, he says, "made much of" and regarded as "an amusing eccentric" because of his Scots accent and pronunciation. Medically, he found that Biochemistry and Physiology were taught superbly and the fact that pathology was part of the curriculum in every year, meant that he was able to perform autopsies in later, army, days. His 21st birthday occurred while he was in Michigan but all too quickly this "happy and enriching experience in tranquil surroundings:" came to an end and he was detailed a ship in which to sail home. Unfortunately, this was just a couple of weeks before he was due to sit his Finals so he didn't obtain his degree from Michigan until nearly 30 years later when he sat with the class of '73. Many of the students of the Rockefeller Scheme became eminent in medicine. 25 became Professors, three Fellows of the Royal Society, three Presidents of Royal Medical Colleges, four knights, one peer, one chief scientific adviser to the Department of Health and one a University Vice-Chancellor.

On arriving home in Scotland Jim attended Glasgow University Medical School for six months or so, because of small curriculum differences, before taking his degree. "Glasgow was excellent for the art of medicine, bedside teaching and other aspects – really I had the best of both worlds in the two countries."

He was appointed Houseman at Glasgow Royal Infirmary but shortly afterwards he was 'called up' and served in the Royal Army Medical Corps for two years, reaching the rank of Captain. He saw service in India as part of 'the romantically named, Royal West African Frontier Force' which had been fighting in Burma. When the troops were due to be demobilised in 1945, he went over to West Africa with them for a brief time. Jim was still in the army after the war ended and it was when he was posted to Shropshire that he met Joan, who became his wife.

After his army service he did a six months refresher course at Glasgow Royal Infirmary before the couple moved to Leicestershire, where Jim worked in General Practice, in Market Harborough, for a couple of years. Then, in 1951, Jim and Joan arrived in Woodhall Spa.

"The village is very different now, as is General Practice" says Jim, "I remember George Armour telling me I must live within a mile of the surgery when I took on the partnership." (He certainly succeeded in this as his house is only some 200 yards from the surgery!) "Woodhall Spa was smaller and quieter, with much less traffic – one of my memories is of driving down the Broadway and seeing a friend driving from the opposite direction. We stopped, wound down our windows and had quite a chat without holding anyone up at all. Tor-o-Moor Road and Alverstone Avenue were not adopted roads so were still just gravel. Many of the roads out of Woodhall were not well made and we knew which because the practice covered a large area – Potterhanworth, near Lincoln in the north and Old Bolingbroke in the Boston direction. Yes, it could be difficult if we were called out to a patient in an outlying village, particularly at night in winter. Once, I remember, Dr. Wallis from Horncastle couldn't get through to a patient near Woodhall because we were cut off by snow. Meanwhile I had a call to a house near Horncastle, so he and I swapped patients on that occasion. In those days patients weren't used to seeing different doctors. There was just Dr. Armour and myself in the practice and a part-time secretary. There was no practice nurse and no emergency back up. We had to be self sufficient with surgeries, visits, home confinements and minor surgery and we were on call every other night and every other week-end. The doctor was very much part of the community and we certainly felt needed! Once, George and I even did an autopsy in the home of a dead man. George had performed them before the war in Horncastle hospital. On this occasion an elderly man had died alone in his flat. He'd had no recent treatment so a death certificate couldn't be issued. The Coroner, at Spilsby, asked if we could do an autopsy so the two of us, with a policeman present, undertook the work. We hadn't been busy long when there was a crash and we turned to find the policeman on the floor – he'd fainted and had to be dragged outside!

There were three chemists in Woodhall at this time. Wokes on Iddesleigh Road, Hubbert's on the Broadway, opposite the end of Stanhope Avenue and the Co-op had a chemist too.

As well as being George Armour's partner in the practice I was his assistant at the Baths. He was doing a lot of good work there and it was very interesting for me.

It is some years now since I retired from active practice, and the Baths closed in 1983, but I have been associated with the Baths, first as a member of the Management committee and latterly as a Trustee of the Bath's Trust, for 50 years. I was employed in a professional capacity in the department of Rheumatology for the first 38 of those years.

When I first arrived in Woodhall in January 1951, my knowledge of spas was limited to a hazy conception of an Edwardian resort where the leisured classes congregated in order to take the waters and stroll through the pinewoods perhaps exchanging the latest gossip and generally waste time.

I suppose the hey-day of Woodhall Spa was probably the Edwardian period – the first ten years of the twentieth century – although it remained active as a traditional spa until the outbreak of the Second World War. Treatments were mainly water-based-immersion baths, various forms of massage under water, the use of powerful jets of water and the application of 'fango' packs which were basically hot poultices of the thick grey mud which was scraped from the walls of the 'adits' – the side passages which fed the spa water to the main shaft of the well. As time went on, more exotic treatments were introduced, including early forms of electrical therapy, and an unpleasant type of enema called a 'Plombiere,' the use of which was based on the theory that some rheumatic diseases were caused by so-called 'toxins' arising in the bowel – a notion which is now completely discredited.

It should be remembered that spas were used to treat many conditions beside the rheumatic diseases – everything from skin diseases to 'women's complaints,' chest troubles to psychiatric ones. Even as late as 1951 when I came on the scene, there was an 'inhalarium' where spa water mixed with various medicaments such as adrenaline, was vaporised and inhaled in the treatment of asthma and chronic bronchitis. Adjoining this facility there was a rather sinister appearing chamber – completely windowless and lined throughout with marble terrazzo, called the 'fog room.' In the middle of the floor stood an apparatus rather like the jet spray that you fit on the end of your garden hose, the purpose of which was to produce a thick fog of vaporised spa water. It was thought that breathing this mist was in some mysterious way beneficial for your chest. I should add that these relics were soon to disappear.

Of course, in Edwardian days, the social aspect of life at a spa was considered as important as the medical treatment, and the hotels vied with each other in trying to attract the most illustrious clients. The local newspaper published a sort of 'Court Circular' giving details such as, for example "The Margrave and Margravin of Wurtemburg attended by their personal staff have arrived at the Victoria Hotel to take the waters at the Spa," and so on. The 'hoi polloi' had to make do with boarding houses, a considerable number of which were built, and can be seen to this day as some of the semi-detached properties in Victoria Avenue, Iddesleigh Road and Tor-o-Moor Road.

Incidentally 'taking the waters' was meant literally and involved drinking large quantities of spa water each day. If I tell you that one of our problems in designing a special type of tank for water-assisted exercises was the corrosive effect of the water from the well on ordinary cast-iron pipes, you will understand why this was never one of the most popular forms of treatment; in fact the water tasted disgusting, and drinking it was abandoned in about 1936 in the Spa itself, although there was still a 'bottling room' in 1951, and small quantities of bottled water could still be bought in a few chemist's shops, including Wokes in Woodhall. The baleful effect of the water on pipes was also the reason that the water was raised from the well by a Heath Robinson system of a large wooden barrel with a movable base on the end of a wire rope attached to an ancient steam engine. Both barrel and engine are preserved in the Museum of Lincolnshire Life."

The late Mr. John Smithson, Senior, made the point that drinking the water came first and the first bathing was done in the open air, before Thomas Hotchkin built the Bath House in the 1830s. Everyone seems to have agreed that it tasted very unpleasant with adjectives such as "very bitter," "very salty" and "horrible" applied to it. The late Arthur Wokes said "the water tasted foul but in those days popular wisdom was that in order to do you good medicine had to taste nasty – perhaps it was good for their souls!"

So life went on its peaceful way, with walks in the pinewoods to vary the routine of treatments at the Spa, or perhaps a round of golf on the new course to help counteract the rich meals offered in the hotel restaurants. The Baths were operational right up to the outbreak of the Second World War in 1939, and there was even an attempt to establish a rival spa establishment which consisted of opening a so-called pump room in a house at the corner of Stixwould Road and Green Lane, an alternative source of spa water having been discovered.

"During the war, the Spa Baths closed and the buildings became an ablutions centre for the forces, a large number of whom were stationed in the village. In 1945 it seemed unlikely that the Spa would ever be reinstated, particularly because medical opinion in this country was moving away from the concept of spa treatment although it was – and still is – as strong as ever on the Continent. However, a number of public-spirited businesses decided to establish

The Spa in its Edwardian heyday. *Lincolnshire Life.*

The empty buildings in 1986. *Lincolnshire Life.*

The pump room. *Cottage Museum Collection.*

a trust in order to set up the Spa again, and gradually patients began to come back to Woodhall.

The advent of the National Health Service in 1948 ensured the future of the Baths, since the Alexandra Hospital and the Spa Baths were both taken over and incorporated in the Lincoln Hospitals Group.

The spa physician was transformed into the specialist in physical medicine, and finally the rheumatologist. George Armour had been appointed consultant rheumatologist for Lincolnshire and was largely responsible for developing the Baths into a modern and forward-looking centre for the treatment and rehabilitation of rheumatic diseases. Over the years we established an up-to-date Physiotherapy Department, an Occupational Therapy Department with 'model' kitchen and bathroom in order to assess patients' ability to live at home, and a social worker's clinic to give financial and other advice. After a few years, we managed to persuade the Health Authority to construct a deep Hydrotherapy pool, which was done in an ingenious manner, by taking the roof off an underground brick-built water storage tank, which was originally constructed to conserve the spa water in case of a drought, in the days when spa water was considered to have almost miraculous curative powers. At the time when the Spa was first established, much importance was attached to the fact that the spa water when analysed, was found to contain large amounts of iodine and bromine and that the percentages were almost identical with the contents of the famous Austrian Kreuznach Spa water. A great deal was made of this in the publicity of the day, but of course we now know that the chemical content of the water has no curative effect at all. The benefit of submersion in the water, which was heated by steam boilers, was derived from the relaxation of muscles, the relief of pain by the warmth, and the ability to move joints enhanced by the buoyancy of the water. I should perhaps add that one final advantage of using the well water was that at that time, it was free, and no water rate was payable, a fact that was of great comfort to those of us who were on the management committee!

With access to Pathology and Biochemistry laboratories, the provision of x-ray facilities on-site at the Alexandra Hospital and the use of 36 dedicated beds – a luxury enjoyed by few, if any, other Rheumatology units in the country – within a year, the treatment and management of rheumatic diseases at Woodhall Spa had moved from the 19th century to the second half of the 20th. Patients were referred to us from the whole of the county and from many centres in the East Midlands and beyond, including London teaching hospitals. We were among the first centres to be given supplies of the then new wonder drug cortisone, for clinical trials, and I was able to present to a meeting of the British Spas Federation the results of a series of cases of injections of cortisone directly into joints, which at that time was the second biggest trial in the world. Cortisone was very effective at first but it became apparent that after a while its effect decreased.

So what became of the healing waters? By the middle of the 20th century medical opinion was moving away from the idea of spa treatment in this country; it was accepted that the various spa waters had no curative effect at all, and it was felt that treatment could just as readily be delivered in the Lincoln Hospitals complex. At this point I will let you into a secret – for at least two years the regular bacteriological tests which had been made on the spa water for many years revealed that the well was contaminated with a fungus, and so we had been using mains water. Plans were therefore under consideration to close the Alexandra Hospital and the Spa Baths clinic, when fate took charge; early in the morning of 21st September 1983, the brick lining of the upper 100 feet of the well shaft slipped 650 feet down to the bottom of the well, sending a massive column of water with tremendous force up to the surface, causing widespread damage to the wellhead, the boilers, one of which disappeared down the shaft, and the boiler house itself, which was almost completely destroyed. So that was the end of the Spa Baths – shortly afterwards the clinic was transferred to Lincoln County Hospital, and the Alexandra Hospital was closed.

It may seem strange that it has been proved that mineral waters have no therapeutic properties when they gained such a reputation over two centuries – surely it couldn't all be due to the effects of faith. Well, there is one piece of recent research that may explain it. Workers at Bath have discovered that immersion of the human body in fluid of high specific gravity causes an increase in the excretion of lead through the kidneys. Now it is thought that in the 18th century, some at least of the cases of so-called 'rheumatism' were in fact muscle and limb pain due to chronic lead poisoning caused by the lead pipes in universal use. Therefore, bathing in the spa waters may have had some curative effect.

Times have changed and knowledge has increased. How different this village is now from its early days as a fashionable spa and even from the twenties and thirties when a well-known character called Johnny Wield transported invalids around the spa in a donkey cart. He was a lovely old man. I knew him well as a patient in his eighties. He lived in what is now the Cottage Museum – that is very fitting as he was, among other things, an authority on the history of the spa. It was believed that he buried his last donkey in the garden of his bungalow. It is said that if you listen carefully, anywhere in the Spa, you may hear the clip-clop and 'whooshing' sound of the ghosts of Johnny and his donkey cart passing by.

On the other hand, the 'whooshing' may simply be the sighs of relief, emitted by readers who are, at last, reaching the end of this chapter."

Woodhall Spa has been fortunate to have Jim Robertson in its community. An able, kind and hard-working G.P., he obviously could have risen to dizzier heights than practice in rural Lincolnshire. A modest gentleman, he gave of his best, in considered thought, expertise and experience to this neighbourhood, as he would in a grander situation. Apart from General Practice and his input at the Baths, he has served on medical committees, written articles for magazines and for some years was integrally associated with the valuable Training Scheme for General Practice, which began in Boston, Lincs. in 1973. With memories of his two years in Michigan, he was particularly pleased to help with a reciprocal arrangement for young doctors in Boston, Massachusetts.

In the village he is regarded as an erudite, unfailingly pleasant and gentlemanly resident. He was a member of the Golf Club but, as he ruefully points out, beginning play after evening surgery meant there was rarely sufficient light to finish the round! A leisure activity which Jim and George Armour enjoyed together for some years was rough shooting. They took their guns and dogs into the country and shot birds, such as pheasant, partridge, snipe and duck. It was not an organised shoot, the birds weren't driven. In those days before mobile 'phones or two way radios, they arranged with the landowners at Haltham or Bucknall where they shot, that telephone messages would be brought to them. Their wives, at home, relayed any emergency calls they received from patients.

Jim and his wife and daughter, Elizabeth, enjoyed sailing and were founding members of the Lindum Sailing Club in Lincoln. A talent of which not everyone will be aware is his ability as a pianist. Not only is he technically able at playing but he has the gift of being able to play by ear, to the delight of visitors gathered in his home.

Jim still retains his attractive Scots burr and he and his smiling and beautifully turned out wife, still live in the house in Victoria Avenue into which they settled upon arriving here, fifty years ago. They are part of this place and maintain the good manners and courtesy of Woodhall Spa at its best.

Interior of the pump room, 1890s.

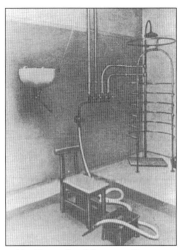

Aix Douche Massage Room.

D. N. Robinson.

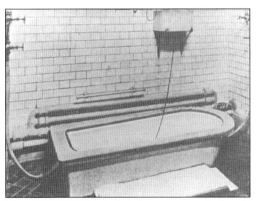

Mineral bath with douche.

Drawing up the water from the well.

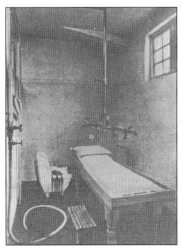

Vichy Douche Massage Room.

Interior of the pump room early 1900s.

Woodhall Spa on old picture postcards.

Woodhall Spa and District Ambulance parked outside the Spa Baths, c. 1940.

Cottage Museum Collection.

This photograph, c. 1960, shows the Spa Baths exterior changed little over the years.

H. D. Martineau.

CHAPTER VI – THE RAILWAY

Cecil Caudle, born 1902,
in a recording of 1988

"My father came from Gloucester to make and repair cycles at Humpherson's shop on Witham Road here. He used to cycle back to see his parents – 170 miles on unmetalled roads!

In about 1915 I started to work in the Baths office, under Mr. Ingham, who was secretary for the Gas, Water and Baths Company. I was paid 3 sovereigns a week with another shilling for 4 hours overtime. The Gas Company office was in Station Road but the works were near Kirkstead Station. It was a dreadful job to stoke the furnaces and even the manager, Mr. Ford, used to take off his shirt to feed the fires in the retort house. Then he had to go out in all weathers to collect money from gas meters.

I have many memories of the old days here. I was a lad of 18 when I held a pump at the fire at the Victoria. It was a waste of time, like just turning on a kitchen tap.

I remember making a crystal wireless set and Basil Kirkby inviting neighbours in to listen to his new, 1 valve, wireless. Before wireless we used to read, by oil lamp or gas light, or play darts – we had a dart board in the kitchen – and there was the piano to sing around and card games like solo or whist.

I was married, at 25, to Ivy Semper who worked at Bycroft's Laundry. The 7am train from Horncastle brought in about a dozen women to wash, dry and iron in the laundry. She also worked as a children's nurse at Horncastle Workhouse for a while. In summer we used to listen to the bandstand concerts, sitting on deck chairs, at 2d a time and being bitten by gnats!

We had our photo taken by Johnny Wield. His studio was a shed in his garden and we sat on high stools. Sundials he'd made were in the garden. I believe they were accurate and he also repaired watches for several people. Posher folk had photos taken by Neale, at "The Vale" in Tor-O-Moor Road. There was a railway poster of a girl in the lily pond of "The Vale". I know that because at the end of World War 1 I passed an exam in Boston and a medical at Kings Cross and began working on the railway – the Great Northern Railway then – at Kirkstead Station, as it was then, selling tickets."

It was in 1922 that the Great Northern Railway agreed to change the name of Kirkstead Station to Woodhall Junction. Woodhall Spa councillors had made the point that first time visitors to the Spa didn't know where Kirkstead was. Squire S.V. Hotchkin preferred the name "Woodhall West" but the GNR opted for "Junction".

The railway was very important to the Spa. Not only for Season visitors but also for neighbouring villagers, some of whom came by train, daily, to work here. The 7½ mile single track from Kirkstead Junction to Horncastle was opened in August 1855. The line was very constricted through the village but a siding was laid alongside the line, west of the Tattershall Road level crossing, in 1887.

"Yes, the railway was very necessary and there were about 6 trains a day from 7am to 7pm. There was also a charabanc to Horncastle but passengers often had to get out to push it up Langton Hill! When it was market day in Boston or Lincoln the platform at the Junction would be thronged with people travelling at the special rate of 1/6d return. Often farmers with goods would be queuing up on the road to cross the swing bridge to the station. There was a charge for farmers with cows and sheep and there were no weekly or season tickets! There were very few cars but they were charged 3d or 6d. Tolls from the bridge were taken to the station, as it was under the control of the GNR. The old way for farmers was to

A wagon marked "Emma S. Lill, Timberland Dales, Lincolnshire" loaded with goods at Kirkstead.

Cottage Museum Collection.

Railway gate and bridge, Kirkstead.

Mr. J. Winter in his garden of the gatehouse, Kirkstead.

transport produce by barges, pulled up the Witham by horses, to grain stores in Lincoln. The railway also had lorries (without windscreens) which collected goods to be transported by train. In the fishing season there were trains of private saloons on Sundays. They were chartered by public houses, in places like Sheffield, on the premise that the anglers would drink their beer. There could be 800-1,000 fishermen and matches were held on the Witham, including the All England Fishing Match. The station was well tended with flowers. Fuller's taxis used to meet trains at the Junction, so there was a choice of train or taxi into the Spa. When it was Tattershall Fair, carriers met the train at that station and took people into the village.

In 1939 I became travelling relief clerk for the 173 London North Eastern Railway stations in Lincolnshire. Stickney was very busy because of bombs and ammunition and East Kirkby because of the Lancasters there. Hundreds of servicemen were travelling by rail at the time the Arnhem raid was planned. I was in Woodhall when the parachute mines dropped. The station was all right but there was a mess, with tickets flying all over the place.

I ended up as chief clerk in the station master's office in Lincoln, doing railway publicity – posters and such. I worked for the railway for 44 years, 11 months and 2 weeks. It would have been 45 years but I missed the last fortnight because my wife was ill. As a result of being off those two weeks I didn't receive my gold watch. I still feel a bit bitter but I think that in the middle of the 20th century we didn't expect as much as now".

Mrs. Riley, née Gladys Winter

"I was born on 25th April, 1923, 2 days before the wedding of the Duke and Duchess of York (later King George VI and the late Queen Mother) Lady Weigall travelled up from King's Cross – she'd been to London to see the wedding presents. Arriving at Woodhall Junction she saw my father at work and said, "Winter, is that baby born yet?" "Yes, madam, a baby girl," "Oh, wonderful, here you are" and she gave him 5 shillings. His wage as gateman at Woodhall Junction was 30 shillings (£1.50) a week.

My father's job was to open and close the railway gates. It was shift work, shared with a Mr. Dalton. There was a hand push gate for pedestrians. Opening the gates for traffic could be trying on wintry nights, after, for example, a dance at Petwood. The bell near the gate would ring in the house and my father would have to get up and dressed and down, to the impatient hooting of horns outside.

There was a garden at the gatehouse which my father enjoyed tending, particularly the roses. At Kirkstead we often won the competition for best-kept station and the diplomas were hung in the waiting room. Mr. Osborn was Station Master at first, then Mr. and Mrs. Pleasance, thought to be the parents of the actor, the late Donald Pleasance. We had a lodger – usually a porter or lorry driver, to help finances. There were 3 of us children and we were each given a penny pocket money on Saturday mornings.

As children we got to recognise and wave to the train drivers and firemen. There were passenger trains during the day and goods at night. My brother sometimes had a ride on the engine when the train reversed up the track to join the line for Horncastle.

The wages were low but there were "perks" working for the railway. There was a free market pass and my mother and I would go to Lincoln on Fridays or Boston on Wednesdays. There was also the "P.T. (privileged ticket) which was about one third of the normal fare and there were 3 full passes a year with which we could travel to London or up to Elgin in Scotland. For years my parents had a short holiday in Aberdeen because they could get there for almost nothing!"

Swing bridge at Kirkstead.

The platform, Kirkstead.

The notice on the platform reads: "Woodhall Junction, change for Woodhall Spa and Horncastle and for Coningsby and Midville Line."

Under the swing bridge, back row left to right: Mr. J. Winter (gateman), a surveyor, Mr. Hubberd (station master), Mr. Dalton (gateman), Harry Moore (porter); centre: Italian prisoners of war (they painted the bridge); front: possibly three maintenance men.

River Witham with the swing bridge at Kirkstead.

Kirkstead station yard.

Cottage Museum Collection.

The station was responsible for the heavy swing bridge across the Witham. Mrs. Riley remembers a toll of 1d to walk across, 3d a motor bike and 6d for a car but this was removed shortly before the war. Barges came up the river from Boston to go to Lincoln. Often after the barge got through the bridge it would pause and Mr. Winter would be given a bag of cockles or mussels. Similarly, farmers would often give potatoes or a vegetable when the gates were opened for them. "People looked after each other in those days", Mrs. Riley reflects.

"I went to the National School until I was 14. I was caned twice – once for talking and once for bad writing! Well, I think my writing's as good as most peoples now!

My first job was with Hundleby's, the grocer over the Witham at Martin Dales. I remember pouring sugar from the cask into 1 lb blue bags. I never could get the hang of those paper cones for sweets!

Then I worked in the Kinema, during the war, when I was 20 or 21. I worked at the cash desk and Tay Crookes took the night's takings, while Major Allport was away in the war. Every night there were queues of servicemen and often they couldn't all get in. Aircrews from Petwood were booked in as a crew, under the pilot's name. I served Guy Gibson once – not that he'd remember the likes of me! There used to be a box on the wall, half way up the hall, pointing towards the cheap seats at the back, with "silence please" written on it!

Pathe News was shown and it was strange to watch war news with so many servicemen who saw it first hand. I used to leave the Kinema at about 9 o'clock at night and walk home. It was pitch black in the woods and there were soldiers everywhere but I never had cause to be alarmed. Sometimes one would see me through the woods to Station Road and I would walk on to Kirkstead.

The station was very busy during the war years. Supplies for the army came in and were collected from the Goods Yard. There were trains to Lincoln early in the evening, which returned late, so that soldiers billeted here could go to anything on, or the pictures, in Lincoln. I stayed at the gatehouse with my mother until the end of the war but then my association with the railway ended, when my husband and I took rooms in Horncastle.

Mrs. Betty Cox, née Gaunt

Betty Gaunt came to Woodhall Spa, as a child of 3, in the mid 1930s. Her father was a railway signalman who was born in Mill Lane but was working in Spalding, where there was onerous night duty. He was pleased to return to Woodhall Spa when the opportunity arose because here there were only daytime shifts. Then came the war and consequently the need for night duty here too!

The family lived on Witham Road and Betty went to the National School. "I remember dancing with Mrs. Belton. We wore dark skirts with slit sides for it. Sometimes Lady Weigall came to see us. We were a little in awe of her with her dressy clothes and make-up and her hair – some people said it was a blonde wig that she wore. She gave us all sweets – that was before we knew about tooth decay and putting on weight and "unhealthy eating".

Betty's mother was second parlour maid for Mr. and Mrs. Hotchkin at the Manor House. Sometimes Betty was taken there to visit her godmother "Auntie Alice". Being good at dressmaking, her mother often altered clothes for the late Faith Hotchkin who was very slight and therefore had difficulty in finding dresses which fit. "If I was there I was always given milk and chocolate finger biscuits. Faith had a little terrier, called "Ratty", that I was allowed to pat. At Christmas we were given a duck or a goose and after she died I was given a pale blue dress with silvery diamanté as a memento."

Woodhall Spa station
platform

Cottage Museum Collection.

A train steams into
Woodhall Spa station.

Woodhall Spa station and the Broadway.

Betty's father worked shifts of 6am – 2pm, 2pm – 10pm and 10pm – 6am with two other signalmen and a relief in case of illness. After the Station Master, the signalmen were reputedly the highest paid. Betty has a small weekly payslip, dated 8th July 1945, which reads "T. Gaunt. Income Tax deducted 4 shillings. Wage £4-5-11d net. His uniform was provided.

It was, of course, a very responsible job. The signal passed from station to station by a system of bells. When the train left the station the signalman would ring the appropriate bell to say so and what type of train it was. There was a code of bells and another informed the gateman of the approaching train. Sometimes a Morse code "tallygraph" (telegraph) message was sent between stations. Other railway employees were platelayers and line walkers. The latter was, perhaps, an unenviable job, walking along checking the line in all weathers, carrying hammers and spanners. "We knew them all and there were characters like Skinny Miller who was always cheerful and wore an open shirt whatever the weather.

We took the trains for granted when I was young. Everybody used the railway – trades people, the ordinary people of the area and grander passengers as well. I felt quite sad when they decided it had to be run down. It was part of Woodhall Spa".

Passenger trains at Woodhall Spa stopped running in September 1954, then, with the cessation of goods transportation, Woodhall Spa lost its railway altogether, in April 1971.

Recorded recollections of Arthur Wokes, chemist and his son Paul

"After Mr. Collins died I bought the premises on Iddesleigh Road, so I was in Woodhall Spa from 1939. I was on the parish council, a chairman of the committee which organised a hall for the village (Coronation Hall). Many people gave their services to that, such as Mrs. Flury, who raised money and Frank Knowles who worked for Kirkby, the builder.

I was also general secretary of the ambulance committee – there was a real need for an ambulance in the Spa. Harold Howard was working secretary, a rough diamond but practical, modest and unselfish. He was shot at the end of the war.

At the other end of the social scale there was Stafford Hotchkin who was very good for the village if, sometimes, a bit out of touch with the common herd! Mrs. Boys, the doctor's wife, was a real aristocrat and a very good chairwoman. There were many "good neighbours," such as Rev. Taggart who was vicar of St. Peter's from 1952-76. He was a genuine Christian. There was Jas. Belton at the school. Now he could be a bit fiery and wasn't always appreciated but he was very sincere and a really good teacher. He got some of us to talk about business to the 14+ children who were due to leave school, which was quite a new idea. Also he organised English classes for The Poles who were here during the war. Many of them couldn't speak the language.

A war time memory which has its funny side but which could have been serious, occurred during the black out. It was evening and pitch black – no moon – and I was meeting someone at Woodhall Station. Standing on the platform I put my foot out to see how near the edge I was and fell onto the line!"

"I was born during the Second World War. I liked to help in the shop but on Saturdays, when it was busy, father would get rid of us youngsters by saying, "take this wire (or wood or material) to Johnny Wield next door." Johnny was a very inventive man and found a use for anything! When we arrived he would show us his shed and bath chairs and photographic equipment or anything he was working on. He was fascinating to listen to. He was known as the timekeeper of the village and people went either to him or the station for the correct time!

I remember the trains. My younger brother often received a tip for opening the gates near Johnny's, for people to go across the line. When he was a bit older he'd hang around there and as the train slowed down for the station he could jump on to the driver's cab. When the train arrived he would help to open the double gates that went across the road.

In the shop, it was before the time of screw top bottles. Corks can go fusty, so bottles from the manufacturers were stored, without them, in the cellar. When they were soon to be needed the bottles were washed in hot water and drained and then a paper disc was placed over the top of each to keep them clean until they were filled with medicine and corks put in. "Washing and papering" was quite a skill and, as a teenager, I could do two or three hundred in an afternoon. Of course, there were far fewer proprietary medicines in those days."

Walking in the woods, a popular pastime even today.

CHAPTER VII

Reminiscences of Mrs. Priscilla Coriat, née Weigall, recorded shortly before her death in 1996

Priscilla Crystal Frances Blundell Weigall was born on 18th April 1914, a few months before the outbreak of World War I. Her father, Captain, later Sir, William Ernest George Archibald Weigall, was a grandson of the 11th Earl of Westmorland. Her mother, Grace Emily Blundell Maple, had inherited a fortune from her father, Blundell Maple, of Maple's famous London furniture emporium. There was thus a happy combination of titled background and wealth.

"Yes," said Priscilla, "family connections were considered important when my parents were married, in 1910. Sometimes my mother's great friend, the Princess Marie Louise, herself a grand-daughter of Queen Victoria, would joke, "But Grace, darling, you're trade!"

In fact, despite not being of aristocratic birth, Grace was a Baroness prior to becoming Mrs. Weigall. She had been married to the Baron von Eckhardstein, well known German ambassador and friend of the Kaiser, with whom she had a baby daughter, Kathleen. However, the marriage was not happy and Grace divorced the Baron for adultery and cruelty.

Priscilla Weigall as she appeared in the society papers after the announcement of her marriage to Viscount Curzon.

"She was terrified of him," exclaimed Priscilla. "He used to beat her with chains. I believe this was the first time a lady had given cruelty as grounds for divorce."

The baroness had been visiting Woodhall Spa, staying at the Victoria Hotel, for some years before the divorce and had built a house in a favourite spot, calling it "Petwood."

Interestingly, her grandfather, the founder of Maples, had named his home in Horley, Surrey, "Petridge Wood".

"I think my parents met at Blankney, where my father was land agent for his cousin Hugo, the Earl of Londesborough. After their marriage they lived at Petwood with Kathleen, "Kit," as she was called. I adored her but, sadly, she died when I was only 3. She was nursing during the war but needed a minor operation from which she didn't regain consciousness, despite being under eminent London surgeons.

My parents had a life-style that was part and parcel of Edwardian and pre-war times. There were dinners and balls and house parties all the time. My mother needed people the entire time. She loved entertaining and sometimes there would be 30 or more sitting down to a meal. There were shooting parties and cricket weeks and always people, people. There were holidays at fashionable places – Le Touquet, Aix les Bains for the races, polo at Cannes – with the ladies dressed in the latest fashions. One thing about my mother was, perhaps, rather surprising. She was pretty but she was wicked about having her picture taken – only snapshots. I can't tell you how bad she was and she flatly refused to have her portrait painted.

My mother loved grand people but she was interested in and generous towards everybody. Sometimes my father muttered a bit about her spending but it was often for the benefit of

Sir Archibald and Lady Weigall with Mrs. Baldwin.

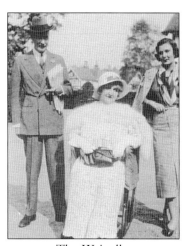

The Weigalls.

Miss Priscilla Weigall and
Lord Curzon at Petwood.

Priscilla Weigall, Viscount Curzon, Lady Grace Weigall
and Sir Archibald Weigall, Petwood House, 1934.

Sir Archibald Weigall, Governor of South Australia,
with the Prince of Wales.

Lady Weigall with John and
Peggy Flury.
Cottage Museum Collection.

others. Of course, my father fitted in very well in the social scene but it wasn't important to him. He was passionate about agriculture and was entirely a countryman. He loved pottering about in old clothes but was dragged into social life by my mother. He was an M.P. for a quarter of a century and it was a great delight to him, when they had the big house in Hill Street, in London, to invite M.Ps from every political party to dinner. As well as the well-known Tories he was a close friend of Aneurin Bevan, Ernest Bevin and Herbert Morrison and at least one <u>burning</u> Communist.

Of course, they argued in the House – that's what the party system of government is for but they respected each other. It's such a shame the way Parliament has become with all that bickering and spying. I mean, who cares who sleeps with whom? Men have always had affairs. It was a wonderfully enriching time for me. My father would greet me from school and say "put your satchel down and come and see who I've got in the study." Perhaps because I met so many people I became a Socialist later on and once, when I was married to Curzon, I was speaking in Bolton Town Hall and Aneurin Bevan, in the audience, shouted out, "Lady Curzon it's about time you changed to our side!" He was a prominent Labour politician, of course. Grace didn't altogether approve of some of these visitors but she was friendly with some of the wives. I remember Mrs. Baldwin, the Prime Minister's wife. She was a funny old girl and persuaded my mother to go shopping in Woolworth's with her, to buy trimmings to give a new lease of life to her hats!

These times were built upon the foundation of my wonderful childhood in Woodhall Spa. The country-life has stood me in good stead. All the village people were so kind. I used to talk to them all and the staff at Petwood were my friends. Mr. Greenfield, a gardener, was a lovely old man and my father's Australian groom was a real friend to me. I used to go riding with my father at 7 in the morning, across those endless fens. Once, when I was about 8, my father noticed me constantly turning to look back. An old lady in the village had told me to watch out because some day the sea would come roaring up behind me. I was really frightened but my father said "Nonsense," very firmly and we rode on! I had a pony and trap when I was 11 or 12 and there were lots of animals – too many animals what with horses and dogs and rabbits. I used to go for walks and cycle furiously along to the village and help at harvest time. At Petwood there were 2 good hard tennis courts and well-known players like Silva D'Oliveira and Helen Moody sometimes came. Then there was the swimming pool, oh and I had a battered old boat I used to row on the lake. As long as I was tidied up to meet my parents in the evening they didn't care where I'd been. There were other children my mother made sure I met, as well as those I came across in the village. I remember Neil Hotchkin, of course but he wasn't always around as he went to Eton. Every now and then my mother would take it into her head to hold a party for me. I hated these dressed up occasions but Grace loved organising them and fussing over the children."

The party scene is vividly described by Miss Maddison of Partney, who was one of the junior "social set." "There would be about 30 children brought in their big cars and at Petwood we were met by a footman in livery and our coats were taken by a maid. There were lots of servants about. Lady Weigall swept in, making an entrance. She wore a lot of make up and looked like a pretty doll. Sir Archibald seemed rather nice and ordinary. We used to play charades and Grandmother's Footsteps (when you had to freeze when "grandmother" in front turned round) and there was dancing and tea, of course, served by maids in little white frilled aprons and caps. I think Priscilla preferred the outdoor life to being indoors among all the lavish furnishings. She was my age, I was born in July 1914, a week before the outbreak of World War I. The first time I met her Lady Weigall swept down on us and said "Well, Priscilla, have you asked this little girl to your party?" I must have been considered suitable! Or perhaps she was giving her daughter a social prod! Lady Weigall was beaming, indulgently but Priscilla looked rather cross! She had a strange, rather lonely life, constantly being paraded in front of a stream of visitors.

Of course, the Weigalls were newcomers here and their society lifestyle seemed a little flashy but they had the interests of the village at heart and no-one doubted Lady Weigall's generosity. Even after having to use a wheelchair, after slipping on a pavement, she kept her enthusiasm for everything and everybody."

Priscilla continued, "I didn't have any formal education until I was about 14 but it was a wonderful childhood of country life and working people – far better than mincing around in velvet with my hair tied up in ribbons!

There was an awful lot of drip when I was a deb. Grace was in her element but I loathed being social."

Priscilla was a debutante, presented to King George V and Queen Mary in 1932, when she was 18. There were fulsome reports in the newspaper about her – Daily Mail. January 1932, "Who will be the prettiest deb of '32? My choice is Miss Priscilla Weigall. She is radiantly lovely with dark brown hair and eyes and a complexion which a woman described to me as the most perfect she had ever seen. She is a fine dancer and swimmer and equally popular with men and women friends." Evening News. June 1932, "Lady Weigall and Miss Priscilla, who looked lovely in a white lace dress with a big spray of flowers, attended the Derby Eve Ball, after dining at Grosvenor House with others including the Marquis and Marchioness of Northampton." Yorkshire Post. June 1932, "Rose of Empire Ball at Grosvenor House. Three of this year's most important debs., Lady Pamela Smith, Miss Priscilla Weigall and Miss Nica Rothschild were there." The News Chronicle, in May, described Priscilla's suite of rooms, which included a guest bedroom, at their home, Englemere, at Ascot, which the Weigalls had bought when they decided to make Petwood a hotel. The Sunday Times, in July, wrote a report of Priscilla's coming out ball, describing it as "to be long remembered." Lady Weigall had supervised everything, even until midnight the night before when she was helping to wire foliage to trellis in the garden. A "charming beer garden" had been created and, inside, the house was full of "quite lovely flowers." Lady Weigall "regal in a white dress, was seated at the top of the stairs in a massive crimson and gilt chair, with her wheel chair behind. Priscilla was in white satin. The guests included "many titled aristocracy and 3 princesses." On a lighter note, amidst all this lavish splendour, the Sunday Graphic reported a clash of parties. Lady Cunard was holding a French Evening at the same time, on the same evening, on the opposite side of Grosvenor Square. Both houses had striped awnings at the door and guests driving up failed to look at the numbers of the houses, went to the wrong one and had "to trail across the square in the heat when they found out their mistake!" At the actual presentation, court procedure, by which a debutante was escorted by one parent in front of their Majesties, was waived and Lady Weigall was "granted the privilege of passing their Majesties in the throne room in Buckingham Palace in a wheeled chair," with her husband.

"Woodhall Spa was terribly special to me. It tore my heart out when we left. After my parents had decided to pass Petwood over to John and Peggy we still stayed there and had weekend house parties before it became a hotel. There was one time, in 1933, when Pongo Clydesdale flew over to see me, landing in a field near the house. He took a girlfriend and myself up in the plane. He had flown over Everest in a single engine Tiger Moth and the film of it was shown in the house and at the Kinema – oh, that unique Kinema in the Woods, such happy times. Clydesdale wanted to marry me and Grace was absolutely flipping over it because he would be a Duke but I didn't want to marry him.

He was a dear friend, a brave, sweet man and he was good looking too – in fact he would have been more fun than my first husband! But I didn't want to be that grand."

Alterations were made to Petwood before it opened as a hotel. More bathrooms and a gym were installed and one wing of the building was organised for children and their maids, with a playroom equipped with toys and books. But, only a year after opening, disaster struck in the form of a fire which caused severe damage and destroyed one wing of 18 bedrooms. A report in the Evening Standard of 27th July 1934 said that fire had broken out in an unoccupied bedroom over the kitchen. The housekeeper, Miss Bannister, informed Mr. George Garner, night porter, who fired a rocket to alert the Spa Fire Brigade. Guests helped firemen drag furniture outside and villagers turned out to help. Dr. George Armour reported flames nearly 50 feet high. Sir Archibald and Lady Weigall, who had just returned to London, were in bed when telephoned with the news. They were still shocked but relieved when, later, they were told the fire was under control. Almost exactly a year after this, Priscilla, married Viscount Curzon, son of the 6th Earl Howe who was first cousin of Curzon of Kedleston Hall, Derbyshire, one time Viceroy of India. A newspaper described the Viscount as being "very good-looking, as befits his lovely mother and beautiful sister, not to mention his exquisite Alfa Romeo"!

"Curzon's father was a racing driver so he grew up loving cars. He often drove to Woodhall Spa and his wedding present to me was a car. Curzon was on the L.C.C. He was elected with a majority of 100 after a recount over Douglas Jay."

The wedding took place in the chapel of St. Michael and St. George (the order of which Sir Archibald was a knight) at St. Paul's Cathedral. National press coverage was extensive. The Yorkshire Post described it as "one of the most spectacular, socially brilliant weddings of the generation, with over 1,000 guests." The Morning Post described Priscilla's white and silver brocade dress with its square neck and long train ending in 3 points for the 3 small bridesmaids. She wore a diamond and aquamarine pendant and matching tiara which held a white, intertwined with pale blue, tulle veil. Pale blue tulle was the material of the dresses of the small bridesmaids while the 4 older wore pale blue crêpe, shot with silver. The Standard of 27th July 1935, devoted a whole page to the wedding, commenting on the many distinguished guests, the dense traffic which stopped crowds outside St. Paul's and the fact that there had been a special train from Woodhall Spa to take "hundreds of Lincolnshire folk" to London. Apparently, Priscilla arrived 10 minutes early at 2.50pm and sat with her bridesmaids at the top of the steps of the cathedral!

"Yes, it was a society event with several Royals present but it was wonderful that so many people from Woodhall Spa were there. I have a wedding book full of signatures, oh, everybody signed it – Greenfield the gardener and Lickorish the chef at Petwood, John Wield from the cottage – that's the Cottage Museum now, – Allports, Armours, Overtons, the Misses Lunn from the school, Mrs. Roslyn from the china and fancy goods shop, John and Peggy Flury, of course and many more. I still treasure it. Really I had too much of Royalty when I was young. Curzon was a godson of Queen Mary and it was a terrifying experience when I became his fiancée, when I was just 20 and I had to walk along a slippery floor of a long room at Marlborough House to be introduced to her. She looked severe but actually she was very good, loving and kind. When I ran away and married my 2nd husband she was frightfully understanding and the present Queen Mother was exceptionally nice too. When my parents lived at Ascot, she and the late King George VI – lovely man I adored him – sometimes invited them to visit at Royal Lodge and they had an entrée to Buckingham Palace. They used a side door there and were taken up in a lift with the wheelchair. I have some letters from the present Queen, as a girl, to my mother. Then there were the Kents, lovely Marina, across at Coppins and others, such as the Duke of Norfolk sometimes stayed. The Prince of Wales visited us when my father was Governor of South Australia. I was 6 when we went there. He talked quite freely with my father. Of course, he charmed the pants off everyone but his heart wasn't in kingship. In the late Twenties, long before Mrs. Simpson, he wrote quite hysterical letters to my father saying he had no intention of being king and was going to abdicate. She was just the catalyst. I gave the letters to Windsor Archives after my father's death in 1952.

I was nursing during the war and I had a Guernsey refugee living with me. She worked in a factory and I looked after her children. We had lots of East End refugees at the Old

Gardens and south front of Petwood before it became a hotel.

Another view of Petwood in winter.

Huntsman's Lodge at Windsor Park – it really belonged to the Royals, I rented it. The refugees arrived and I de-liced them. There was such a wonderful, pounding pace to every day and I felt I was doing something to justify my existence. Being social and "coming out" was all so empty, stupid and idiotic.

Howe (Visount Curzon) made a happy 2nd marriage. I sometimes visited them. I married my 2nd husband in 1948 and was widowed in 1970. I've been living here in Farmington (near Cheltenham) for 20 years. Such exceptionally nice country people, I don't live a social life or see any of the Royals now, of course. I haven't for years. I last visited Woodhall Spa in 1975. So many changes, so many memories. Neil Hotchkin was still there, very busy with the Golf Course and Sandy Armour, I remember him as a schoolboy, was a G.P. in his father's old practice, while he, "Georgie Porgie," was still helping at the Rheumatology Clinic. I stayed with Peggy Flury for a month, such a good friend, from solid North-country stock. We talked about the old times and the war years at Petwood and the characters. Guy Gibson was a wonderful man. Whatever their backgrounds there was a special relationship among the men. Some were so young, 18 and 19. Sometimes they were in tears before setting off."

Reputedly, Grace would have liked a son and heir for Sir Archibald but this was not to be and she had died before her grandson, from Priscilla's second marriage, was born.

"He is a barrister and legal adviser to the British Governor of the Turks and Caicos Islands in the West Indies. I had 2 daughters when I was married to Curzon. It is interesting to me, thinking of how my father and I loved country life and Grace adored gardening, that one of my daughters, Mary Keen, is a well-known garden consultant and writer."

Indeed, Lady Weigall loved colour and flamboyant displays of flowers and also the design of a garden, with which she had been so involved when Petwood was built. Once, after a trip to Malta, she created a "Maltese garden" at Englemere, with hanging terraces and Maltese crosses as part of the flower beds. When the Hill Street, Mayfair, house was bought, an artist was hired to paint scenes of Petwood gardens, terrace and rose garden, on walls of a room.

The story turns full circle, for at the end of the 20th century, Lady Mary Keen was invited to Petwood to give a talk on gardening to the Lincolnshire Gardens Trust Council. She was surrounded by the rhododendrons, shrubs and lawns which her grandmother had created almost 100 years before.

Mrs. Peggy Flury
who, with her husband John, turned Petwood into a hotel.

"We first knew Grace at the beginning of the Thirties. She and Sir Archibald would take a suite for a couple of weeks at our Hotel Washington on Curzon Street, Mayfair. Then, one time, she said, "My house, Petwood at Woodhall Spa, has been empty for four years, why don't you come and make it an hotel? We'd never thought of such a thing but, in the end, she got her way. We'd never even been to Lincolnshire!

We'd just got turned round when we had that dreadful fire. We never knew exactly what happened. The Weigalls had been up and they always brought so much with them. For a start there was always Grace and 2 doctors and her maid, Priscilla and her maid and Sir Archibald, his valet and the chauffeur. This time they were going off to Australia and had brought all their wardrobe to be packed, although they had to go back to London that night. The servants had the new part of the building and all Priscilla's frocks were laid out in layers there. I think they must have been careless, hobnobbing together and someone dropped a cigarette. It was awful. We were closed for six months and weren't insured for loss of profit. Luckily the front of Petwood was undamaged but we had to rebuild and refurbish a whole wing of the hotel."

Recorded memories of Mrs. Linskill, née Wright.

"I was born in 1905 and when I was fifteen I began working in service. After two years I became cook at the Dower House, here in Woodhall Spa. I would have liked to work here sooner, but, in those days, you had to stay in one place for two years or you would have no character when trying for another job.

The Dower House had been built for Mr. Stafford Hotchkin's mother and when she died it was bought by Mr. Eaton Evans, estate agent for Sir Archibald Weigall. The Eaton Evans treated us well. We ate the same food as the family and our afternoons were free. As well as myself there was a kitchen maid, housemaid, parlour maid, chauffeur and a woman who came in twice a week to clean. We began work at 6.30am. I remember there were twenty-two copper doorknobs and eleven locks to be polished each morning! In the evening, dinner was at eight and then there was washing up etc. until ten o'clock or so. I was paid about £1.10shillings a month (£1-50p). We didn't meet any visitors, of course, but we sometimes saw them from the front kitchen window. I saw Princess Marie Louise go past once. She was a regal sort of lady – well I suppose she would be, wouldn't she?

I remember Johnny Wield's donkeys were kept in a little field between the railway and the Dower. I nearly fell off my bike going to work early in the morning when they suddenly started to bray!"

The drive and entrance of Petwood.

The Dower House, built in 1905.
Cottage Museum Collection.

CHAPTER VIII

Woodhall Spa & St. Andrew's School – Miss D. I. Hopewell Remembers.

Dora Hopewell at her 90th birthday coffee morning party.

In St. Andrew's School Log Book, dated 10th July 1939, is the entry "Miss D.I. Hopewell commenced duties as Supply Teacher, in charge Class IV."

On the same day it was the school's 4th Annual Show of Wild Flowers, with 10 prizes for "arrangement and rarity." The following day it was the 3rd Annual Sports Day. Both of these activities were of interest to the newly appointed Miss Hopewell, as Nature Study and Physical Training were two of her subjects.

The school, with 148 children on roll, broke up for the Summer Holiday at the end of the month but the break was cut short by the recall of teachers on 5th August, in order to prepare for an influx of evacuees from Grimsby, because of the threat of war.

Miss Hopewell remembers the confusion and hard work for everyone at this time and her difficulty because of being a new arrival.

Reception and billeting began on 1st September and continued over the weekend. The entry in the Log Book is brief and basic "Sunday 3rd September. Mr Dee, H.M.I. again visited school this morning. War was declared at 11a.m."

The next day the school was closed but Miss Hopewell recalls all the teachers being there, trying to accommodate extra children and cleaning and masking windows in "Woodlands" on the corner of Broadway and Stanhope Avenue (now Broadway Carpets) which was to be a canteen and social centre for evacuees.

It was on 4th September, also that Miss Hopewell was appointed to the permanent staff.

At this time, St Andrew's School was a building now converted into a bungalow at

Came Court on Witham Road. It was too small to house the extra children, so, on 18th September, it opened, as Miss Hopewell says "on a shift system." Woodhall children attended between 9am and 1pm, followed by the evacuees, from 1 until 5pm. This was, so she says, a relief, after almost a fortnight with 60 children in the class. At first attendances were lower as, in the general alarm, some parents were concerned that there was insufficient protection at the school, if there were an air attack. A few Grimsby teachers had accompanied their pupils here. Mr Belton was the Headmaster and continued to be so until he retired in 1963. His wife also taught at Woodhall until her retirement in 1961.

The children were aged from 5-15. Eleven year olds who were selected, left to attend the Queen Elizabeth Grammar School in Horncastle but there was no Secondary Modern School until Gartree was opened in 1954 – "Sam Leggate was in the first year to go, I remember."

In 1939, after the initial solution of a shift system for coping with all the children, a more satisfactory method was sought, and towards the end of October, a busy weekend was spent organising Woodlands into a department for the Infants and Standard 1. The Infants Department remained there, in fact until the first part of the present building was opened in 1962. There were 4 classes at Witham Road, two of which were in a long room, divided by a partition. A routine was soon established and, hearing Miss Hopewell talk and looking at entries in the Log Book, one has the impression of a caring village school, dedicated to education, religious education and the general welfare of the pupils. Life was controlled, orderly and respectful, and the staff could and had to deal with everything. "There wasn't any classroom help in those days" reminisces Miss Hopewell, "we just had to do it all. Some children walked to school in all weathers and we often had to strip them down and dry them or clean them before we started teaching. We had to see to them if they were poorly and generally act "in loco parentis" as well as teach.

There was milk at Playtime – that was delivered by Mr Robinson – and there were always children needing help with the tops or spilling it! For lunch they brought sandwiches – the Canteen wasn't built until 1948. Once it was built they had an Infants Dining room at Woodlands and food was taken up there in Thermos containers. Mrs Marshall was cook for a long time. After the war we had "Meals Supervisors" and Mrs Pell and Mrs Kent were there for about 20 years.

From the beginning of the war we had to check the children had their Gas Masks. They weren't allowed to stay in school without one if there was a raid. One or two parents wouldn't give them to their children for some religious reason.

Well, if they lived at Green Lane or somewhere like that, a long way off, it was dangerous for them to walk home. After a while people nearby offered to have them if they didn't have a "Government Civilian Respirator" – everybody called them "Gas Masks."

We had to have air raid drills and there was a shelter at the bottom of the garden. It wasn't big enough, so some of us had to shelter in the Church, next door (St. Andrew's Church, of which only the graveyard remains). We used to try to be jolly for the children and I played "A hunting we will go" and such like but once there was going to be a funeral and the coffin was there, so we couldn't!"

By ill chance the first two winters were cold. The lavatories froze up for days and the tanks had to be filled by hand. (The Log Book aptly describes "considerable inconvenience"!)

"Supply teachers came and went and there were often changes. We had a Mr Heywood on the staff and he joined up about the first summer after the war started. About 2 years later he was married and we went to the wedding with some of the Seniors and them, when the war ended he came back to teach. It was strange for him after 5 years in the Forces.

Materials were short in those days and you used anything you could find for writing. For drawing or painting there was wallpaper, even newspaper. Books were precious and couldn't be replaced so we backed them and took care of them and an inventory was taken regularly.

We were expected to teach formally. There was reading around the class and saying tables – quite a lot of learning by rote. The children sat 2 to a desk that had a bench seat attached and they were in rows, of course. They were expected to be quiet and listen (or, at least look as if they were!) and to behave themselves. If they were really naughty they could be given the cane if the teacher had permission for this – there always had to be a teacher in school with authority to cane, usually it was the Headmaster but, if he was away.....Naughty children could be made to stand outside the door for a while or we could tap them on the leg with a ruler but, usually a telling off was enough. Corporal punishment had to be entered in the Punishment Book – I expect there are one or two around Woodhall now whose names are in it!

There were Scholarship Intelligence Tests (later Secondary School Selection), which were taken very seriously. Mr. Forbes, Head of St. Hugh's would come here to invigilate and Mr. Belton went to St. Hugh's.

We always had Open Days when parents could come in and look at what the children had done – there was an Open Afternoon for the end of the school year, just a fortnight after I started in Woodhall. We didn't have work in groups or several things going on at the same time, or children wandering around the room but it wasn't all stiff and repressive. There were lessons like Needlework which were quite chatty and cosy." (The Log Book for 19th August 1940 comments "A new Singer Sewing Machine has been received." This followed the report that the Head and a Prefect had voluntarily treated the windows with Arpco to prevent them splintering from the blast from high explosives.) "As a War Effort children knitted squares to be made up into blankets and older girls knitted socks for soldiers – they were done on 4 needles and turning the heel was always a problem. Whether the poor men ever wore some of them I don't know."

The first air alerts came in 1941 but there was no serious trouble in Woodhall Spa until 1943 when, on 17th and 18th August, 2 parachute mines dropped, one on the Royal Hotel (where "Royal Square" is now). After this the school was closed for a week because of broken windows and ceilings down.

Woodlands was worse with several doors blasted off and it was closed for longer. Miss Hopewell remembers Mr. Dee, the local Inspector, coming in when she was on hands and knees scrubbing the floor. "But that was nothing when you think what might have been" says Miss Hopewell. "Just one week before, there had been a Demonstration – a concert – in the Winter Garden of the Royal and all the Societies – Brownies, Guides, Scouts – just about every child in the village was there. I remember it well because I had to make a speech and I was afraid I'd forget it. I was really nervous and then I was held up setting off and then the railway gates were closed! Anyway I got there and found they had a microphone behind a curtain so I could just read my speech after all! But that next week, when the parachute mine dropped, the Winter Garden was destroyed and there was a dreadful mess next day.

Dr. Armour's house was hit and Mrs. Armour was hurt. I was just down the road from there, with Mary Rose, at Digby Villa (Victoria Avenue). We hadn't bothered with the Air Raid Shelter when the siren went – you got used to it, you know. Well, we heard something and I went to the window and, whoosh! There was such a blast and the roof was gone! We hardly knew what to do but we managed to get downstairs and there were some soldiers next door who said we shouldn't stay there, so we walked to Mill Lane, to Mary's parents-in-law at the bakery. I found myself carrying an eiderdown and a doll! When we got there they didn't know anything about the attack. The best of it was that Mary had been to London just that day, to fetch her niece to stay in Woodhall, to be away from the bombing!

There were soldiers here everywhere in wartime. There was a camp up Horncastle Road, about opposite Sandy Lane. Once there was a march for the Girls Training Corps to go there, from outside school, with an A.T.S. officer. I was Commandant of the Girls Training Corps and had to lead. So we set off and after a while, I thought it was quiet and I looked round – the others were miles behind, I was marching by myself!

There was a lot of activity with the G.T.C. There were parades for occasions like Empire Youth Sunday and the Salute the Soldier campaign. We had Squad Drill and Figure Marching and there was also instruction in Home Nursing and the girls would be tested by a local doctor and given awards.....

Later, I was Senior Officer commanding the South Lincolnshire area of the G.T.C. There was fun as well, of course. Every year we had a G.T.C. Birthday Party – a Social Evening with someone singing, a "potted sports" and a General Knowledge Quiz. We always managed refreshments, despite the rationing. Occasions like this always ended with the National Anthem – it was sung much more in those days, at the end of a film show for example. Then there were the Sports Days for the 859 Company of the G.T.C. – us with Horncastle and Bardney. Mrs. Flury, from Petwood, gave a Cup for that – the Flurys were very good to the village with money and time. She was Chairman of our local G.T. Committee. We had Needlework classes and made our own shorts for Sports Day.

Staff of Woodhall Spa C of E School in 1940, Dora Hopewell is in the centre between
Leslie Heywood and Mr. J. Belton, headmaster.

St. Andrew's School,
Witham Road.

St. Andrew's School
decorated for the
Coronation of Queen
Elizabeth II in 1953.
Cottage Museum Collection.

We held Sports Days in school as well and they were wonderful in Mr. Belton's time. One race followed straight after another without any waiting about. I was in charge on the day and for years Major Allport and Mr. Adcock were the starters. We had every child in the school in a race and they were never crying or cross if they didn't win. There were 3 Houses – Weigall (Red) after Sir Archibald and Lady Weigall from Petwood House, Daman (Blue) after Dr. J. W. A. Daman, a school manager for some years and Harvey (Green) after the Rev. Harvey. At the beginning of the Seventies, in Mr. Cavanagh's time, there was a 4th House – Cheshire (Yellow) called after Group Captain Leonard Cheshire, Commanding Office of the 617 Squadron, who was stationed here during the war. There were beautiful silver cups – one from the Weigalls and one Dr. Daman gave us in about 1940, I think and The Ross Young Cup – that was sad. It was given in memory of a pupil who died. He was in my class and I noticed he was sometimes unsteady or would slip off his chair. I told his parents I didn't think he was right and he was diagnosed as having a cerebral tumour. We were lucky to have the swimming pool so near. During the war the airmen from Petwood used it but afterwards the Weigalls gave it to the village. Later we had swimming Galas with nearby schools and Woodhall usually did very well.

After the war, emergency trained teachers went, as staff came back. There were married women as well – they hadn't been allowed to teach before. I wasn't trained, in the modern sense, when I joined the school – my parents couldn't afford college for me and there weren't grants then. So I went to a Teachers Centre at Bardney, where I lived, when I left school myself, aged 14 or 15. I was there for 4 years. There was 1 year of study with 1 day a week teaching, then 2 years practical and one year of half-time teaching. When I started full time teaching in 1930, I earned £90 a year. Of course, everything cost less then – my board and lodging was 15 shillings (75p) a week. It took 20 years of teaching to be qualified. After I'd taught 18, Miss Watson, an Inspector of Schools, suggested I went to College for 1 year and even if I did nothing I'd be qualified – but I didn't want to do nothing – I wanted to teach!

In the years after the war we gradually had more help in school such as a school Secretary. Of course, there had always been professionals coming in. Educationally there was the local Inspector for Schools, Mr. Dee. He lived in Iddesleigh Road and was a golfer so he always liked to come here in the morning and play golf in the afternoon! He always seemed to ask the children the same questions, often about nature study. I remember there was a tree, a Hornbeam, up Horncastle Road and he always asked the children what it was – I made sure they knew that! As well as Mr. Dee there were various County H.M. Inspectors and, it being a Church School, there were Diocesan Inspectors too. Though I say it myself, they were always full of praise and said the school "was a pleasure to visit." Actually, I was a Methodist by upbringing and I only got the job in a C of E School on the understanding that I wouldn't teach Catechism. The Curate, Father Holmes, came to take that. Well, he didn't realise I was Methodist and, when he was going to be away once, he thought I would take it. He was horrified when he discovered why I couldn't! He was very High Church.

Then there were all the Medical folk who came in – the School Nurse was often in and the Doctor for inspections and especially if there was an epidemic. There was Measles and Mumps and Whooping Cough, and the school closed early for Christmas one year during the War, because of Scarlet Fever. There was the Hair Nurse and the Dentist and someone for eyes and the audiometrician for ears and later, a few years before I retired, there was an Educational Psychologist as well.

Another who came regularly was the "Kid Catcher" as they called them – they could be quite frightening people. I remember, when I was young, I was off school one day, which was unusual for me and the "Kid Catcher" accused me of being at the Lincoln Fair which was on at the time. I was quite scared. Children didn't dare stay away in those days. Later, "Welfare Officers" like Mr. Kirk, who came about 1960, weren't so fierce. He came every

Staff of St. Andrew's with Commander Maitland, M.P., left to right: J. Belton, E. Belton, E. Blades, Commander Maitland, D. Hopewell, L. Holborrow, A. Baker.

Copyright Universal Pictorial Press & Agency

New building of St. Andrew's C of E school when Dora first taught there.

Cottage Museum Collection.

week and checked the registers. Sometimes there were workmen in school, if something wasn't working properly and for years we had Mr. Bridges to tune the piano. Later the police came in, giving Road Safety Talks – we didn't need those when I started teaching – and cycling Proficiency Tests started sometime in the Sixties" In the early years the school was really part of the life of the village and, during the war, there were times, like "Wings for Victory Week," when the school put on a display for parents and villagers, and the school managers and well known Woodhall people, such as Colonel and Mrs. S. V. Hotchkin all attended. On that occasion there was a Poster Design Competition and there were songs from the Junior and the Senior Girls Choirs, both of which were trained by Miss Hopewell, who was also responsible for a Senior Girls P.T. display. The Senior Boys gave a performance of Sword Dancing but it was Mrs Belton, who was in charge of that.

After the war, an Inter-school Music Festival at Horncastle was organised and Miss Hopewell took the choirs to compete in it.

There were also General Knowledge Quizzes held annually among local schools but by that time Miss Hopewell was Head of the Infant Department so her concern was only one of interest. "A wonderful time in the old days was May Day. We chose a May Queen and the children danced around a Maypole. We used to go to Alexandra Hospital and dance there. Mrs Belton organised that. She was very good – it's hard to keep your patience. Some child always drops the ribbon or steps the wrong way and you can end up in a dreadful tangle!

Talking of dancing – we were once on that radio programme "Down your Way." I was in the playground with the gramophone doing Country Dancing with the children (we didn't have a hall so P.T. and everything had to be taken outside.) A van stopped and the team asked if they could interview us. Well, I sent them to the Head, who was at the pool and, after they'd interviewed there, they came back to me – I think they can't have found much in Woodhall Spa! Anyway, everybody seemed to hear about it but when the programme was broadcast all you heard me say was "stop" at the end! We always had plenty of visits outside school. That first November of 1939, we took the Infants and evacuees to see a Meet up at Tor-o-Moor. During the War there were National Savings films and others at the Kinema in school time, and the whole school went there in 1953 to see the film of the Coronation and, later again, we took the children to see the first moon landing film. Major Allport, who owned the Kinema, would invite the whole school if he felt it was something important. It was very good of him.

Apart from local places we took classes to Boston and Lincoln. In about 1948 the school was closed for a couple of days and the seniors with some of the Parents Association (formed in 1946) went to London and visited the Tower and St. Paul's and we had tea at a Lyons Corner House but the big thing was visiting the Houses of Parliament. We were taken round by Commander Maitland who was M.P. for Horncastle. We went to London again for the Festival of Britain Exhibition in 1951 and it was about this time there was an Exchange Week when about 10 of the seniors went to Portsmouth. Afterwards, children from that school came here and were taken to the Wolds and Lincoln. I seem to remember a lot of national events when we had holidays. We had two days off for V.E. Day in 1945 and a day for the wedding of Prince Philip and the Queen. Later, Mr and Mrs Belton and myself took a lot of children to London to see all the decorations for that. I think it was that trip when all the children wanted to look at was the traffic lights! They weren't used to them round here, you see.

The children were usually good when we took them anywhere, although there were always one or two awkward ones and some things were strange to them. I remember one girl – Isobel Wright, she was called – just wouldn't get on an escalator, in London. She'd never seen one and refused to move. In the early days, summer holidays were different. We had a week or so at the beginning of August and a couple of weeks in September/October for the potato harvest when children were helping on the land. They were sometimes off school at other times – for potato planting or beet singling.

The first talk of a new school I remember was after that dreadful winter of 1947. It was very cold and to make it worse the boiler wasn't working properly – the temperature was scarcely above freezing for days. The school bus couldn't get through for a month because of snowdrifts. Pipes were frozen and then, when the thaw came, they burst. Well, it was an old building. At first a new one was planned for the same site with some extra land but that didn't happen and it was fifteen years before the first stage of the present building was opened – just for Infants at first. The rest of the school moved in 1968 and there seems to have been new bits built on ever since!

Oh, yes, there have been so many changes since I arrived, since my first years here. The War really changed the character of the area and particularly of Woodhall Spa. In 1939 it was all Bath Chairs and in 1946 all prams!

In school there were gradually more helpers – dinner ladies, playground ladies, welfare assistants, like Mrs Tidd in the Seventies. There were more materials and visual aids and T.V. We've had decimalisation and different teaching methods, less structure and more "Do it Yourself" learning and there were "Advisers" for a while instead of "Inspectors." I had 3 Heads – Mr. Belton was followed by Mr Marshall in 1963 and then it was Mr. Cavanagh from 1971. I retired in 1975, I can hardly believe it, I was at St. Andrew's for 36 years!

I've seen umpteen changes of staff and there have been different ancillary staff and cooks and cleaners – Arthur Houldershaw who came as Caretaker just before I left was a pupil when I first went to the school. He was boys Vice Captain in 1939!

But, above all, there have been so many children! Some have settled in the area and it's nice when they recognise me and say "hello."

Sometimes I hear about others and it's always good to know if they've done well.

Sometimes it's ones you wouldn't expect and that's encouraging too. It's like having every child in a race on Sports Day – some might not be good runners but they could jump, or throw, or do the Egg and Spoon. Really, teaching amounts to giving a child a basic knowledge and finding what he can do and trying to encourage that. I've always believed everybody can do something. Miss Hopewell retired from teaching at Christmas in 1975. She still lives in Woodhall Spa, her home for 60 years, not far from the old St. Andrew's School, scene of so many memories.

Recorded reflections of Mrs. Eileen Belton
widow of James Belton, Headmaster of St. Andrew's School for 26 years.

"Lady Weigall was always to the fore. At the outbreak of war she stood up in church and her voice rang out "You must all up and do your duty, for war is declared." Woodlands was all prepared to receive evacuees from Grimsby when the Weigalls came round. Lady Weigall set about making "suggestions" and organising everybody but Sir Archibald whispered that we should let her have her say and then do what we'd planned!

I enjoyed doing Maypole Dancing and gym with the children. We had gym displays in the Winter Gardens and I gave dancing lessons all over to raise money for a new floor for the schoolroom. Talking of the Winter Gardens, I remember that night when the parachute mines dropped. Children were brought to the schoolhouse and we had beds everywhere. It's funny how people react. The home of Mr. Hubbert, the chemist on the Broadway, was badly damaged and the family was very shaken. Someone found a bottle of brandy in a cupboard but Mr. Hubbert said "You can't use that, we're keeping it for an emergency"!

Mrs. Win Howsam of Hundleby's grocers

Mr. and Mrs. Howsam were married in 1934, having bought a new semi-detached property on Witham Road. The houses were built by the local firm, Kirkby's and cost about £450.

Hundleby's was opposite the Royal Hotel, on Station Road and Mrs. Howsam recalls, vividly, that night in the war when the hotel was hit by the German parachute mine. "They came to the house for my husband because the shop window was blown out but he wasn't in because he was doing his two hours fire duty. Anyway, when he got there he found much of the stock was on the pavement. The strange thing was that the jam jars hadn't smashed and they were all standing the right way up, as if they'd just been lifted and put down somewhere else."

Mr. Scott Targett, aged 91
in a recording of 1992, former manager of the Royal Hotel.

"I was a Methodist and total abstainer from alcohol, working as a purser with the Cunard line, when I was approached by a Westminster gentleman, Mr. Arthur Harper Bond. He said he had a property in Woodhall Spa which he wanted to make into a conference hotel for workers in the temperance world.

So, I came to Woodhall Spa and a limited company was formed, as capital was needed for alterations and repairs. The place was in a poor state.

My predecessor had had a popular bar and there were half a dozen other places in the village but I abandoned the seven-day licence, refused entry to boys with bottles and stopped pass out checks when customers would have had alcohol somewhere else before coming back to the Royal. I made a loss at first but, after a while, I had a nice clientele.

We had a Boxing Ring and I organised shows with boxers from as far away as Manchester and customers came from Boston and Cranwell as well as locally. I also had a Table Tennis Club for young people and had the National Champion to give an exhibition. Also there were amateur dramatic performances from time to time.

I was part of village life, a manager of the village school (and a great friend of Mr. Forbes at St. Hugh's) and on the Council. I took care not to plan anything, which would conflict with other activities such as at The Kinema. Major Allport was a director of the hotel company.

Then the war came and the hotel emptied. I was food controller for the village and put in charge of the evacuees from Grimsby. I had to allocate lodgings for them – there were about seventy children and they all needed de-lousing first. We met them at Woodhall Junction and Lady Weigall, "Lady Bountiful," was there. She gave each child 6d to buy sweets and said "Go to Mrs. Tyler's for ice creams and tell her to send the bill to me" "Oh, yes, she was generous but she was all show and she interfered. Once, I was talking to Mrs. Hotchkin when Lady Weigall's name cropped up, "Oh yes, she's a draper's daughter, isn't she?" she said.

The Royal had been closed during the First World War but the Army requisitioned it for the second. They came in 1940 after I'd had the expense of black out material. A full inventory was taken and they paid rent but their gun carriers ploughed up my car park and they concreted over my beautiful sprung maple dance floor. We had to feed the Observer Corps girls at 3d a time.

In November 1941 I decided to return to London. I applied to the Ministry of Food and was put in charge of Chelsea and then other London Boroughs. I left Mr. Brookman in charge of the Royal and he submitted monthly reports. When the Ministry of Food folded up after the war I transferred to the Department of Housing and Local Government and was in charge of the City of London. Later I was made a Freeman of the city and awarded the MBE.

I often remember the country life in Woodhall Spa. I was a Methodist preacher and during the war I was preaching when the Arnhem boys came back. The church was full, with extra chairs in place and when I was just about to begin a note was passed to me "please remember the chums we left behind." Of course, I had to scrap the sermon I'd planned.

When the German parachute mines dropped in Woodhall Spa in 1943, I lost everything. I didn't want to rebuild the Royal. A beer garden was suggested for the site but I certainly wouldn't have that, so, in the end, it was given to the UDC in trust, as a memorial to the village.

Hundleby & Co. in the 1950s.

The Royal Hotel, stretching to the crossroads on Station Road.

CHAPTER IX

Memories of Mrs. Joan Monk

Mrs. Joan Monk, née Bennett, was born in Woodhall Spa and has seen many changes over the years, particularly in the shops.

The Dairy lasted longer than most and Joan remembers being sent out for milk, occasionally, when she was a child and having to wait for a large, rosy cheeked, lady to arrive, in a big, horse-drawn vehicle with the urns, straight from the farm. When it was the lily season in the Spa there would be a wicker table outside the dairy, piled high with bunches from the Hotchkin wood.

Memorable characters among the shopkeepers included Mr. McNaulty who mended cycles in the wedge shaped premises next to the station. He had such a broad dialect as to be almost incomprehensible to Lincolnshire lads and lasses.

Mr. Bourne the butcher, in the present Papworth's shop, also had a fish shop on the Broadway. His wife didn't serve but took the money and did the accounts in the shop, always wearing a hat.

Another lady with a hat was Mrs. Best. Best's, on the Broadway, always stocked fine furniture, some of which, on fine summer, pre second World War, days was put outside on the pavement. Mrs. Best would be seen there, be-hatted and smiling at potential customers and passers by.

There were several shops selling ladies clothing, including Mrs. Kent's and Miss Orpen's. The former lady, on Station Road, kept a large stock of corsets, vests, bloomers etc. haphazardly arranged with several items hanging above the counter. Mrs. Kent was not tall and bobbed up between the garments in order to serve her customers. Miss Orpen, on the Broadway, stocked beautiful clothes from London, with an exclusive dress or outfit in the window. Inside, however, the shop was rather a muddle and Miss Orpen often had to look for something among boxes piled in the back. Display was generally not given much consideration in those days.

Many shopkeepers obtained goods from London. The 9.10am train from Woodhall Spa, with one change at Woodhall Junction, arrived at King's Cross at 1pm. Three hours later, the 4pm from King's Cross was back here at 7.30pm.

Bryant's was a shoe shop on Station Road for many years. If a customer's requirements were not there, Miss Needham would ring the main shop in Horncastle for the desired shoes to be sent on the bus. The cost of the 'phone bill was unimportant compared with pleasing the customer.

Mr. Setchfield was a barber on Station Road. As a girl, Joan remembers her father collecting his car in the morning from Fuller's garage on the Broadway – she remembers a Morris Oxford with a dickie seat – and driving down to Mr. Setchfield's to be shaved, before setting off to his work as a seed merchant.

Joan went to school at Hartington House when Miss Joaquim, successor to Miss Lunn, was headmistress. She was part Malaysian and a very dramatic sort of person. Emphasis was laid on clear speaking and the girls had regular exercises in articulation and elocution. An activity which Joan thought was great fun, in the Thirties, was Living Whist. This was performed in summer, in the garden of Petwood, on the grassy square in front of the "temple." The playing cards they were representing were shown on the front of their costumes but their backs were plain blue so they would not be known when shuffled. There was a table in each corner and, after shuffling, they were dealt to a corner, where they remained until their card was called – Joan was 10 of Clubs. Then they would move to the Joker in the middle, who

The Conservative Club.

Cottage Museum Collection.

Mr. Setchfield's. Later he moved lower down, on the other side of Station Road.

was all dressed up and with a hat with bells, to discover who had won the trick and therefore where they should go. Joan thinks it must have been worked out beforehand and it was certainly very clever.

In 1946 a play reading group in the Spa was suggested and Joan and her husband Stephen, were among the first dozen or so members. The main movers were Pat Carson, a teacher and his wife, Nell. The group met weekly in each others houses.

The following year the group became "Woodhall Spa Dramatic Society" and performed three, one act plays, which were directed by Hugh Martineau, a teacher at St. Hugh's, at the Womens Conservative Club. At this time, the Conservative Club was housed on the Broadway, where Forbuoys is now. Men played cards and snooker in the upstairs rooms while the women's rooms were downstairs and were much used for whist drives, with some very keen lady players. A narrow entrance led from the Broadway, with the "box office" on the right and then doors into the room. The premises stretched back almost to the railway line and could accommodate a large audience. The plays were well received but the actors seem to have had even more fun from their rehearsals and performances. There was an open invitation for anyone to join the group, on the understanding that it was light-hearted entertainment for members, although complete professionalism was the aim in performances.

There was some difficulty in finding places to rehearse. There was St. Hugh's Gym or the Golf Hotel Ballroom or the room used by the British Legion off Witham Road. This was before St. Peter's Church Hall was built, of course.

The Conservative Club was not ideal for performances. On one occasion an actress found beer was dropping on her head from a spill in the Men's room above! Also, the exit right, had to be through the lavatory window, achieved by standing on the loo! This could obviously be very tricky if there wasn't much time or the costume was bulky. One hesitates to suggest that parts were allotted for size rather than suitability!

A more civilised setting was Petwood Hotel where, for a few years, beginning in 1947, Peggy Flury asked the group to perform some cameo sketches on Xmas Eve. After these performances they were provided with a splendid meal.

The first 3 act play was in 1948, "Night Must Fall" by Emlyn Williams. It opened with a completely black backdrop and Wallace Monk, Stephen's brother, dramatic with his imposing voice and white judge's wig against the black. Margaret Smith, now "Bunny" Game was in this play and Mollie Jordan, a well-known member of the Golf Club, was property mistress and prompter.

The Society was fortunate in its helpers. There was Jack Overton who was marvellous with the stage, which often needed enlarging. He might be there until 4am upon occasion – the room wasn't empty for him to start until after midnight. David Clench, who taught at Horncastle Grammar School, designed wonderful sets and Sleight and Crooks, a local firm of decorators, helped. There was furniture from Roslyn's, which was on Station Road and other local shops – the Dairy, Laura Fowler, the Gas Office, would take programmes to sell. The cast themselves cajoled friends into lending suitable props. Inevitably, there were expenses, such as the printing of programmes or hiring of costumes and when the society moved to the Coronation Hall for its performances, expensive stage curtains had to be bought. Any profits were given to charity.

The plays ran for three nights, jolly events attended by most of the village, with coffee served in the intervals. For some years two plays were enacted, one in spring and another in November or December.

A very successful production which Joan remembers was "Bonaventure", in November, 1957. During one performance there was the sort of hiccup which can so easily occur. She was on stage and supposed to answer the phone when she realised it wasn't there! Luckily,

Dramatic Society – left to right, standing: Nell Carson, ?, ?, Stephen Monk, Pat Ireland, Pat Carson; seated: Joan Monk and Phyllis McNiff.

Dramatic Society production of "Bonaventure" – left to right: Joan Monk, Mollie Jordan and Gwen Stuart. The costumes were blue with black aprons.

Nell Carson, acting the part of charlady, brought on the telephone quite naturally saying "sister, you'll be wanting to answer this." Apparently the slip went unnoticed.

In the 1960s Woodhall Spa Dramatic Society closed the curtains on its final play, to be restarted as Woodhall Spa Drama Group in 1970. This had happened more than once during the twentieth century.

Looking at advertisements in programmes one is struck by changes of the last fifty years. In 1951 Laura Fowler was advertising "Wools, Men's Socks, Ties, Gloves, Shirts and Pullovers, Layettes and Children's Wear, Luxicots and Kamella Rugs". The same programme carried a 5-stanza poem advertising The Casket, 10, The Broadway, which began:

> "Your watch has stopped, your clock won't go
> This has happened before you know
> The only thing to do just then
> Is bring it in to Number 10"

In 1955 the Lime Tree Cafe, long time occupant of the premises of the present Chinese Restaurant on the Broadway, advertised Morning Coffees, Afternoon Teas, Sweets and Cigarettes, while Annie Long, on the Broadway, was selling Suits and Millinery with Outsize a Speciality. The same lady, a year later, advertised, in addition, Gowns and Coats and Stocking Repairs."

It is heartening to note, in these times of constantly rising prices, that one thing remained the same throughout the first 10 years of the Dramatic Society's existence. The price of a programme was sixpence (6d which would become 2½p after decimalisation) from 1947-57!

Jack and Joyce Dowse, Tattershall Road

"We built this bungalow in 1961 and moved in after we were married, two years later – we'd been courting for sixteen years. We had a few days in Scotland for our honeymoon. I don't know how we found the way, as I'd never been out of Lincolnshire. In fact, I haven't been anywhere since, except with work to Warrington," said Jack.

Jack and Joyce were both from farming families. She from Bracken-Woodside Farm, since demolished to make way for the Bracken Golf Course and Jack from Halstead Hall, Stixwould. His grandfather had bought the Hall, 2 cottages and 200 acres of land from Neal Green, in 1945, at a cost of £12,000. Mr Green had restored the Hall, which is a sixteenth century building on the site of an earlier, moated, house. It is brick with decorative stone work and impressive bay windows. After his grandfather's death Jack's father and family moved to the Hall. He remembers their furniture being transported by horse and dray.

"I worked on the farm – an eighty hour week – and had two shillings and sixpence pocket money. Then, when I was about twenty-one, I got £2-10-0. I was better off than Joyce, though – she worked for her father for nothing!"

I bought a bike as soon as I could. It was a Rudge, costing seventeen shillings and sixpence in Lincoln. After I'd bought it I cycled home behind a bus because I didn't know the way until I got to Horsington!

Nostalgically, Jack and Joyce recall times when house doors were left unlocked, when Woodhall Spa was full of gentry, when milk was taken by pony and trap from Jackson's farm on Abbey Lane, to be sold in Robinson's Dairy for one shilling and a halfpenny a gallon. Mrs Hotchkin used to drive around the village in her Austin 7, without feeling obligated to indicate which way she was going and stop outside Hundleby's, where an assistant would rush out to take the order and bring the required groceries to the car.

"She was wonderful, a different class, of course, in those days but it was natural to her and she was so kind. She said she would give me a cow once and insisted on having it brought round to me," recalls Joyce. "Another character was Dr. George Armour," says Jack. "He would come to us, at Halstead Hall, on his bike or motor bike and he liked a bit of sparring (he'd done some boxing) when he arrived. Sometimes I did some work in his garden. He had us plant potatoes at the side of Tasburgh Lodge, where his son, Sandy's bungalow is now. They were to give to his poorer patients."

"Famous people used to come to Petwood which was near our farm," Joyce continues. "Gordon Richards, the jockey, used to stay there if he was racing at Lincoln. He would give us a tip for a horse but we never dared risk the money! Once I saw the king - George VI - when he came to see the troops during the war. It was by the Bowling Green on King George Avenue. They walked in those days, with bodyguards, of course. There were soldiers and airmen all over during the war. There must have been ten to twenty thousand of them. Soldiers got a bit bored and would practise shooting at our milk churns and the Dambusters, at Petwood, would come to the farm to see a bit of country life. Sometimes a chicken went missing but it was fun!

I remember one airman who was desperate to milk a cow but he missed the bucket and got milk all over his trousers! Then he had to rush back with no time to change before they took off!"

"The airmen used to come to Halstead to buy petrol from us – we had a good ration for the farm. It was 11½d a gallon then and you could buy twenty gallons of petrol, ten cigarettes – Woodbines – and a box of matches for a pound! In those days, if a bill came, to say, a pound and a penny, they would only charge a pound, to thank you for your custom. My tractor was often useful during the war. When the Royal Hotel had to be demolished I took the stone for a shilling a load, a lot of it for Mr Would who built on Stanhope Avenue and Horncastle Road. I used a load of rubble from the hotel to build up the drive at Halstead.

After Dunkirk we had five thousand soldiers billeted at the Hall, in the house, outbuildings, crew yards, fields and under hedges! They were pathetic to see and it made us realise how lucky we were in Woodhall. Mind you, that first morning when my father and I went to milk the cows we had to search everywhere to find them!"

617 Squadron 'Dambusters' Memorial.

Woodhall Spa Tourist Association.

CHAPTER X

Mrs. E. E. Allport
and the Kinema in the Woods.

The cheerful, friendly and sprightly figure of Eva Allport has been seen around Woodhall Spa for many years. For she was born here, Emma Eva Bycroft, on 23rd April 1918, just over 6 months before the end of World War I. Two months after her birth it was reported that Ration Books were ready to be supplied to the nation. In August, in Woodhall Spa, a Bank Holiday Fete was held in aid of the Red Cross and the War Hospital Supply Depot. The evening dance was curtailed because of an air raid warning.

Mrs. Eva Allport, 1997.

Eva's grandfather, a Yorkshireman by birth, had started a hand laundry on Tor-O-Moor Road, where the antique firm Edmund Czajkowski and Son, is now. This was a sensible enterprise in view of the large amount of household linen required for the hotels and boarding houses of the Spa. An advertisement in the "Horncastle News" on 2nd January 1909 reads:-

"Yorkshire Laundry
Woodhall Spa
Est 1889
William Bycroft
(Proprietor)
No chemicals used
Extensive open-air
drying grounds."

Another, later in the month, states, "the laundry cart visits the Red Lion, Horncastle, on Saturdays from 12 noon to 3pm. Anyone wishing to send laundry by carrier can have the same returned the following Saturday". Mrs. Linskill, née Wright, who was in service at The Dower House in the 1920s, worked in the ironing room of the laundry for a while. She recalled that it was very big and very hot with four girls ironing there from 7am to 7pm. She remembered the beautiful tablecloths from the hotels and the difficulty of knowing the heat of the old flat irons and how awful it was if you scorched a cloth. From the profits of his laundry, grandfather Bycroft was able to build two houses on Witham Road, one for each of his sons and it was in one of these that Eva was born and lived for 21 years, until her marriage in 1939.

"There were 3 of us children – I had a brother and a sister – and the house was next to where the Fire Station is now. It was all fields then, the village was much smaller and we seemed to know everybody. My father was a builder – "Kirkby & Bycroft" – they were a well known firm " They were indeed. The newspaper of 9th September 1911 notes that the important contract to build an entire new wing on the Spa's flagship hotel, the Victoria, had been secured by Messrs. Kirkby and Bycroft, for £1,100. The census of that year listed 1,635 residents in the village. "I suppose my childhood might seem boring to today's children with all their toys – don't they have a lot of toys? And so many educational things, from being babies, and T.V. and videos. We didn't even have a wireless. We made our own games that didn't cost anything, like Hopscotch .... well a bit of chalk .... no, we often just scratched the squares on the ground with a stone. Then there was skipping and you might have a proper

Bycroft's Laundry, c.1906.

D. N. Robinson.

Weigall Clinic.

Cottage Museum Collection.

The Mall at the Royal Hotel before it became the Winter Gardens.

rope with wooden handles but a bit of old washing line, knotted at the ends would do. There was almost a season for different games, partly the weather I suppose. You would see somebody with a top and whip, then everybody would be out with them. Some were like cones down to the spinning point and some were mushroom shaped and they were painted pretty colours. It was safe to wander round the village in those days and we would press up to the shop windows like Roslyn's china and antique shop which was where the library is. Woodhall was really alive in the Season and we liked seeing the fashionable clothes of the visitors and hearing funny accents but when they'd gone it was our village again. We didn't often leave it. There was the Sunday School trip to Skegness once a year but not much else that I remember – no holidays away. I went to the Wesleyan Chapel on the Broadway. The Bycrofts were big Methodists.

Mr. Thompson was Head of the National School when I was there. I can't remember how many teachers there were. Mrs. Maltby came from Horncastle I think to teach singing. Once it was "Jerusalem" and perhaps we weren't trying very hard, for she said "You know you should learn this one, it will still be around when these other songs are forgotten." There were visitors to the school sometimes, as well as the vicar and nurse and the like. Lady Weigall used to come and she would give us rides on the back of her wheelchair. We played hockey at school. My friend was Kath Shaw. We were in the Brownies together – Renee Osborne was Brown Owl – and then the Guides. Meetings were held at the old Conservative Club on the Broadway. But we weren't often out of the house on winter evenings. Looking back it was cosy with the coal fire and gas lighting. We didn't have electricity, my grandmother wouldn't hear of it!

I left school when I was fourteen and went to work in Rosie Patchett's cafe (now King's newsagents). Her father had a milk round in the village. It was all home-made cakes in those days and there were sweets at the back of the cafe.

My sister worked at the Kinema and when she left I went to help out – so I had two jobs! It wasn't hard work there – I had to tear up the tickets – I thought it was a grand job – by working there we saw all the films for nothing! My father always liked the Kinema and used to go twice a week and see both films. After a while I was promoted to chocolate selling! We had a discount of 2/6d (12½p) in the pound because we sold them. Years later my husband and I were invited to Cadbury's at Bourneville because we'd sold their chocolates for so long. There was a special train from Lincoln for all the good customers in this area and when we got there we were taken round the factory and given tea and some chocolates to bring home. I think we must have been dealing with them longer than anybody else because we were given a lot of attention and I was introduced to Peter Cadbury. Then, we were put right in the middle of the front row for the photo. I still have it here, 14th March 1962.

It was when I was selling chocolates at the Kinema that I met my future husband but, of course, he was "the boss" then. Oh, the Kinema was such fun in those days. You met everyone there, and, as well as the show there were competitions for the audience, such as putting films that had been shown, in order of popularity. Capt. Allport could tell that from the attendances, of course. They would pay 6d (2½p) or so to enter the competition and proceeds were given to a good cause like the hospital. Patients from the hospital used to come to the first house when they were well enough. There were serials as well in those days and afterwards everyone would be talking about what they thought would happen next. Of course, that was the idea of them. They always finished at a really exciting part so that everyone would come back next week! I remember "Rin Tin Tin" went on for ages!

I'd been chocolate selling for a while when they started to do "Living Whist" at Petwood. It was quite a craze in the village, organised by Miss Marshall Hill who lived at Miss Crook's house in Victoria Avenue. There were 52 people in it, of course and we were dressed up for our playing cards. I was the six of diamonds. The kings and queens were very grand with scarlet and ermine trains and they did a stately dance, a gavotte, I think, while the children who were the small cards did jollier rollicking dances. Well, I wanted time off from the Kinema to go to Living Whist but Captain Allport wouldn't let me, so I decided to leave the Kinema!

I went to work at the Weigall Clinic for a while – that was opposite Petwood, on the corner of Stixwould Road and Green Lane. I did all sorts of things there – answering the telephone and seeing to people and preparing mud packs as well. Lady Weigall used to come for treatment herself. She was always larger than life – very charming but she wanted things done her way. "Now don't put my pearls in the sun, will you?" she used to say. After a while the Clinic was transferred to the Baths. There was another massage and treatment clinic which was doing well at the time. It was run by Mr. Hardy, on the corner of Iddesleigh Road and Broadway, opposite St. Peter's and the Methodist Church. Anyway, at the time the Clinic moved, Captain Allport was needing help in the office at the Kinema so I went back. There was a lot of work, arranging for postage, records and accounts to do, noting the films in the book (a certain percentage of what was shown had to be English) arranging the transport of films and collecting them from Horncastle, it was quite a business.

So, with working together in the office, Captain Allport and I got to know each other. He was a lot older than I was and I expect that impressed me a bit at first, when the romance started. We didn't "go to the pictures" like other couples – we were there already and that was work! We used to go for walks and swimming, sometimes in the sea and often in the pool at Skegness. There wasn't a pool at Woodhall then – well not a public one. Mr. Forbes had one at St. Hugh's School and he was generous with it. For a time several of us went there, early in the mornings. It was unheated and sometimes very cold! Mrs. Young, the churchwarden's wife used to go. I remember one day when she was cycling there, with just her swimming costume under her coat, it was very windy and her coat wasn't fastened properly ..... very shocking in the Thirties!

Captain Allport was always keen on physical fitness. He sometimes cycled here from Yorkshire. Yes, he was a Yorkshireman. His parents had the Post Office at Conisborough, near Doncaster. He was a member of the Conisborough Aeronautical Society. I have a medal he was given by them, dated 1910 and a photo of the members flying model aircraft. They do look funny with their caps but Noel Allport looks even funnier – he's wearing a bowler hat! He came down here in 1911 and went to work in the Estate Office at Petwood for Captain Weigall. Then World War 1 came and Noel became a private with the Lincolnshire Regiment. He went to Lincoln Barracks and found 3,000 men in accommodation intended for 150 and only 1 blanket for 3 men. Before they went off Mrs. Weigall gave each of the staff a little silver heart on a chain which they could wear on their waistcoats in those days. I still have it. It has "Petwood 1914," on one side and "God Bless You," on the other. Noel fought in France and in the Dardanelles but was invalided home with dysentery "before the end of hostilities," as they put it. "The next year he was made Commandant of the Southern District school in County Cork and made Captain. Then, after a spell he came back here, to the Weigalls.

Sir Archibald and Lady Weigall, as they had become, were in Australia from 1920-22 and, when they came back, the Spa wasn't doing so well. The Pavilion, on their estate, was near the Baths and Pump Room and the Bandstand and the Victoria Hotel, before it burned down, just 2 months before the Weigalls left for Australia. The Pavilion was a pretty, wooden building with a verandah looking over tennis courts and croquet lawn and gardens. Anyhow it was used for concerts and when they came back Lady Weigall had the idea of turning it into a cinema, the latest thing, so to speak and something else for the village, so they applied for a licence and everything was organised."

A report in "Horncastle News," on 26 August 1922, reads "At Horncastle Police Court, Mr. C.S. Eaton-Evans (agent to Sir Archibald Weigall) applied for a cinema licence for the

Pavilion on behalf of Lady Weigall, to provide a cinema, which was "a crying need" in the Spa." This was granted for 1 year including Sundays.

In his "Book of Horncastle and Woodhall Spa," David Robinson describes how a corrugated iron shed was built onto the Pavilion. Films were to be projected from the back onto a translucent screen. The picture produced was described as being "rock steady" and "the finest in Britain or America. "Yes, that's right and there aren't any overhead rays with back projection", said Mrs. Allport. "David Whyles was projectionist and he stayed for many years".

The opening night for the new venture was Monday, 11th September 1922. The doors were to open at 7.15pm and the show begin at 7.45. The newspaper advertised "an excellent programme at the "Pavilion Picture House, Woodhall Spa." Seats were to be 2/4d, 1/6d and 8d (including tax) for this opening night. In fact, the chosen film, "Lion Eaters," failed to arrive and a Charlie Chaplin was shown instead. It was announced that profits that night were to be given to the Alexandra Hospital. It was a memorable evening for Woodhall Spa and would be a glamorous event, with patrons and Captain Allport wearing evening dress, as they did in those early days. Sir Archibald Weigall gave a speech, in which he commented on "the absence of cheery optimism," which he and his wife had noted on their return to this village from Australia. He hoped the cinema might cheer everyone. It was to be open on weekdays at first but he hoped, eventually, on Sundays too. He commented that "if the people would not go to the church then they must take the church to the people and much good could be obtained from the right kind of film".

"Well, that wouldn't go down well with Captain Allport," remarked Mrs. Allport. "He refused to open on Sundays or Good Fridays. It was against his religious beliefs. He was a churchwarden for years, the Vicar's warden. I think he worked under half a dozen vicars here. I didn't know about profits going to the hospital either. In fact, what profits, I wonder? We didn't make our fortunes from it!"

The new cinema was not, in fact, the immediate success that had been anticipated. Just 5 months after it opened there was a stern reprimand in the newspaper. "Unless attendances improve the Pavilion Cinema will have to close." The cinema had been open during Autumn and Winter. Perhaps people were unwilling to go out, very likely facing a long walk, there and back, after a hard day at work. The population of the Spa was not large to fill the seats and it wasn't the time of year for visitors to be here. Workers wages were low and the cost of outings had to be carefully considered. Whatever the reason for poor attendance it appears that the new picture house had not caught on. However, in June, it was announced that the cinema was to continue, as the financial loss had been mostly from the early days.

Every week the coming attraction was advertised in "Horncastle News." On 21 July, 1923, it was "The Sheik," a Paramount film controlled by the Haymarket Syndicate. Interestingly, there was at first, no mention of actors in these advertisements. Perhaps the notion of "film stars" had not yet arrived. The plot was described in detail, almost to the extent of rendering an actual visit unnecessary. The author was given due credit, for example Edgar Wallace with "Crimson Circle." Then, by 1925, actors were named. On 4th July that year Buster Keaton starred in "Sherlock Holmes," billed as "The Greatest Comedy of the Year." The following week it was to be Mary Pickford in "Tess of the Storm Country" and, on 8th August, Harold Lloyd in "Girl Shy." From the late 1920s Captain Allport gave details of coming films in his "Woodhall Spa Kinema Monthly Gazette."

For these silent films of the Twenties a pianist was engaged to give a background to the action. In Woodhall, Mrs. Tyler from the sweet shop, doubled as Kinema pianist and Mrs. Allport remembers a Janet Enderby who also played. In addition there was "the phantom orchestra." Some cinemas had organ accompaniment and in his delightful book, "The Kinema in the Woods," Edward Mayor describes how, in 1984, James Green, owner of the

The original Concert Pavilion in Edwardian days.

E. Mayor.

Very early days.

Before March 1925, still Cinema but new front added.

Now the Kinema.

Cottage Museum Collection.

Kinema, rescued an old Compton organ and installed it here. It has three keyboards, various sound effects and is lacquered in red and gold.

"Talkies" or "See & Hear" films arrived here in 1930. "Yes, Mr. Whyles was here for the first sound projector to be put in and it lasted 25 years!" said Mrs. Allport.

After becoming a cinema, The Pavilion was still used as a concert hall and for performances by the recently formed amateur dramatic society, which, reportedly, had Rev. C.H. Bellairs as its "conductor".

The first announcements dubbed the building the "Pavilion Picture House" and then the "Pavilion Cinema". "I don't know when or why it became "Kinema in the Woods" but it was before my time there," said Mrs. Allport. I suppose Captain Allport thought "Kinema" was unusual and would make people take notice, though, of course, local folk knew all about it already. It was very pretty round there in those days. There were trees and bushes where the car park is now – there was always the possibility of tripping over a tree root on your way in! There was a lovely path, "Lover's Walk," which went round the building at the back and there was honeysuckle growing up the side of the building." In fact, it was in the mid 1920s that it was referred to as "Kinema," and in March 1925 an article reported that "wireless apparatus has this week been installed in the Kinema, to give audiences the opportunity to listen in for half an hour before the performances begin." It was two years since Mr. Basil Kirkby had installed the first "wireless receiving set in the Spa, since when several aerials have appeared." "Oh yes, I remember Basil Kirkby, he lived on the corner of King Edward Road and he would invite people going past to try his earphones." The Newspaper article reported that there had been continuous improvements to the Kinema in the past twelve months, "despite poor attendances throughout the winter." Then came another rebuke, "If the Kinema opens next winter there may be only one programme at the latter end of the week. Woodhall Spa is the smallest place in the country to have a Kinema with a regular programme of two films a week. It will be a pity if it can't maintain this boast in the future." On 26th September 1925 there was notice of "free admittance to the Kinema tonight on producing today's "Horncastle News."

"After we'd been seeing each other for some time Noel and I became engaged and the engagement lasted two years. Shortly before we were married he received a telegram saying he'd been promoted to the rank of major. We were thrilled but we were specifically told we mustn't tell anyone. It was just before the outbreak of World War II and we had to keep it secret – it was difficult! Later, when my sons would say I couldn't keep anything to myself, I'd remind them of that!.

We were married in July 1939. Despite the threat of war – it was declared less than two months later – everyone seemed really light-hearted. There were so many well-wishers in the village. I treasure a silver salver which we were given by the Urban District Council. Noel became a councillor in 1926 and served for years – 34 altogether! Signatures of the others are engraved on the salver. There is S.V. Hotchkin, Woodroffe Walter, J. Wilson, oh and Messrs. Forbes, Pell, Targett, Fuller, Wheat and Roslyn and Mrs. Page and Mrs. Flury.

We went to live in "Sylvanhay" on Victoria Avenue but we had hardly any time before Noel was called up. He was put in charge of a camp of internees on the Isle of Man. I stayed here and took over the Kinema. Two or three of the men were still there – Charlie Johnson who showed people to their seats and Fred Crooks and Carl Copeland who stayed late until the place was cleared, Ron Webb was projectionist then, he worked at the Kinema for a long time and there was Sheila Bycroft who was there for many years from 1943. It was awful if there was a problem so we couldn't start. Noel was always able to stand up and say something to the audience while they worked to get things right at the back but I was dreadfully nervous. The first time I had to do it I'd just been to the dentist to have three teeth out and I couldn't speak properly. I know I sounded strange because my sister heard me and she guessed what had happened! I had to go to Horncastle to collect the films and that was sometimes difficult with the men away – not so many women drove in those days and there was petrol rationing too. Once I got a lift with Colonel Hotchkin. I think he was going anyway but he just said "Hop in, I'll take you." I felt a bit shy but he was very nice. Well, we managed to keep the business going and Noel came home occasionally.

He was well thought of for his work as Camp Commandant during the war. One of his camps was used to receive Norwegians who escaped through Sweden. The Governor of the Isle of Man, Earl Granville, who was brother in law of the Queen Mother, organised a reception for Crown Prince Olaf of Norway. Noel was presented to him. Oh, it was quite a do and I had to have a new dress – that wasn't so easy in those days. Later, Noel had a letter from the Crown Prince thanking him for the "excellent treatment" the Norwegian soldiers had received.

There was a burglary at the Kinema during the war. Builders had been in to do some repairs but as well as that they took out the safe! That sort of thing did happen in wartime. People needed something putting right and they were glad to get anyone in to do it. Then, often you didn't notice something was missing until it was too late. We lost some small stuff and a mirror that way once. Anyway the police came about the safe. It was only a small one and it was found – opened, of course – in Coal Pit Wood.

It's funny how life is. I know its an awful thing to say but in fact, the war turned us round financially. People came to the Kinema because they wanted to be together and to have some light relief and there was Pathe News in those days before we could see everything that was happening in the world on television. We had our own generator, too, so that the show went on even if power was cut elsewhere. We often had a full house – 365 seats then with 2 showings most nights. War time films were "The Cruel Sea" and "Angels 1-5" but I remember stars like George Formby, Laurel and Hardy, Betty Grable and Ginger Rogers and Fred Astaire with their dance routines. Soldiers stationed here used to come and the airmen at Petwood. Sometimes they saw reconnaissance films, shot over Germany in the afternoon before they went on raids later in the evening. The Weigalls still came even though they'd left Petwood. They had been great attenders over the years and often brought people who were staying with them, well known people and aristocracy. It was always a big do when the princesses, they were grand-daughters of Queen Victoria, came. Princess Marie Louise loved films and she would sometimes come twice in the week for the change of programme. Mrs. Ron Webb, wife of the projectionist, remembered sitting next to Princess Marie Louise, occasionally and being offered chocolates by her. We didn't have the sort of royal box the princess was used to though! The most expensive seats were the deck chairs at the front, the first half dozen rows or so. Once Princess Marie Louise said to my husband – rather pathetically, I think – "Please could you put me somewhere where I won't be kicked?" I suppose if people crossed their ankles when they were in deck chairs .... I don't know where we got the chairs from, they were especially wide ones but I don't think they were made just for us. In the Fifties they had to be taken out because there were new regulations and seats had to be fixed to the floor. Behind the deck chairs there were tip up seats – people used to stub out their cigarettes on the backs of those and they had to be changed after the war. Like many places, there was damage after years of accommodating helmets and gas masks and rifles." The newspaper report of 20th April 1946 said that all the seats except the 2/9s had been replaced and were very comfortable although there had been no rubber available for armrests. "Yes, the prices of seats altered over the years and of course, in the early days there were just forms at the back, uncomfortable but the show was the same!

If the Weigall party was late the show would be held up for them and then they would sweep in and down to the deck chairs. Lady Weigall had a wicker chair at the end of the row and her wheelchair was next to her in the aisle. As well as society folk, politicians, sportsmen and stage people and the like, there were often local friends with them – Dr. and Mrs. Boys and the Bartons who lived at Westerley when it was a private house. Oh, we were always interested to see famous people who were with them. I particularly remember Gracie Fields – her films were always popular and she chatted and was very nice.

There were pegs for coats along the sides of the Kinema – well, they are still there. We wanted to make it homely so local people would feel it was their place. They entered into it then more than people do now and there were so many classic films made after the war and great stars – names which have lived on." Indeed, for a small place, the Kinema then, as now showed all the important and latest films. In one week in May 1948, there was Noel Coward's "Bitter Sweet" with Jeannette McDonald and Nelson Eddy, followed by "Great Expectations" with John Mills, Valerie Hobson and Jean Simmons. "Oh yes, there were memorable films and the audience was quite affected by them – upset by "the weepies" and excited by adventures. In the Twenties there was "Epic of Everest," which was the account of an expedition which reached within 600 feet at the top. Noel said people could hardly believe it – they weren't used to documentaries and pictures of remote places the way we are from T.V. Then, in 1953, it was "The Ascent of Everest," when we knew more of what to expect but there was the excitement of the climbers getting to the top. We put on a show of that in the afternoon for the schoolchildren. My husband often did that. During the war there were National Savings films and such and then there were national events, like the Queen's Coronation, which he put on for the children to see. Audiences were less when television came in and Noel and I used to drive to the villages nearby with publicity posters. That served a useful purpose for me because that's where I learned to drive, on our Lincolnshire country lanes.

Oh, the Kinema was our life really and my husband ran it for 51 years – 1922-73. When he applied for the 50th licence he was given it free!

Noel was very much part of village life, on all sorts of committees and doing this and that. He was Chairman of the Urban District Council three times, in 1934, '35 and '59 and, as well as the usual things with that, he took an especial interest in the freeing of Kirkstead Bridge from its toll." The freeing of the bridge was quite a saga. As early as October 1909 an item on the agenda of the council was "further consideration" of the problem. On that occasion Mr. Overton said that the Great Northern Railway Company would not give up the bridge without payment. The problem was that, being a swing bridge, there had to be someone on duty day and night. It was agreed that more information about the cost was needed. From becoming a member of the council in 1926 Mr. Allport worked to get rid of the toll which he felt was "like a cancer in the life of the place." In November 1927 he suggested that a letter be sent to the government saying how the toll "blighted trade and the development of the Spa, as well as being inconvenient" and that some Road Fund money should be allocated to freeing the bridge. He suggested that copies of the letter should be sent to the County Council and that they should continue to be delivered monthly until something was done! The freeing of Kirkstead Bridge from its toll was eventually achieved – in 1938!

"The Baths Trust was another committee on which Noel served and he was Chairman for years. In 1924 a public meeting was held in the Kinema (still "cinema" then) about the Baths. Sir Archibald Weigall had been keeping them going for 2 years. The Kinema was full. The paper said afterwards that just about every Spa resident was there. They were asked for donations, Noel gave £15 – quite a lot then. The U.D.C. took over the Baths in 1926 but the Baths Charitable Trust was formed 29 years later." The Baths Trust is still in existence, with funds which can be used for medical purposes.

"Noel was really interested in the village and full of ideas. He and two others talked about starting the British Legion here. They were standing round the old coke fire in the Kinema. Anyway, it happened and he was Vice-President. He helped St. Peter's a lot and really pressed for the raising of £10,000 that was needed for the building of the church hall, in the 1960s. With his interest in sport he was a Vice-President of the Cricket Club and founder

The Kinema.

Cottage Museum Collection.

Deck chairs at the front of the house.

Eva and Noel.

Kinema staff in the late 1940s, early 1950s, left to right: Ron Webb (chief projectionist), Sheila Bycroft (2nd projectionist), Major Allport, Mildred Matthews (rewinding girl) and Wally Cooper (electrician).

Lincolnshire Life.

member and first Treasurer of the Hockey Club and Captained it for years before becoming President. Our son, Patrick has his father's love of hockey and played for the County.

We had three sons and they all went to St. Hugh's and have done very well. We felt Mr. Forbes was a good Head and he worked hard to get the school going and achieve a high standard.

My husband's family was spread all over the world and his brother, Denison, who worked for the Bank of England, organised a family party, a "Victory Reunion," after the war, in 1946. Allports came from South Africa, Australia, New Zealand and America to a hotel in London. There were 66 out of 95 known Allports there. I have a copy of the family tree dating back to William the Conqueror. Apparently, the name was "À la Porte" until the fifteenth century.

Noel had been talking of selling the Kinema for some time before he died but he was reluctant to let it go. He died in 1973, the day before our 34th wedding anniversary. My sons saw to the business after he died and they sold it to Mr. Green . His family owned cinemas so he knew all about it.

I was away at the time of that Radio 4 programme about the Kinema, in 1999. "Flicks in the Sticks" they called it which was what it was nicknamed years ago. The programme mentioned that the noise of rain on the roof was a problem when the "talkies" came in. Noel used to say that they never thought of that when they converted the Pavilion but the corrugated iron roof was so good they kept it, even when the building was changed from wood to brick.

It was also said that few of the early conversions still show films. So, if the Kinema continues long enough it might be the earliest in operation, as well as being unique for its back projection! I hope so. We both gave much of our lives to the Kinema in the Woods and to Woodhall Spa but it has been very satisfying, very rewarding to be involved with the life of this village over so many years."

Ken Whyles,
son of David, projectionist at the Kinema.

My father came to Woodhall Spa in 1922 – the year I was born – because of the Weigalls setting up the Kinema. My father was part of a company which worked all over the country and Sir Archibald must have heard of it.

So my father installed the projectory in the Kinema and Sir Archibald installed us, with a shop, in the Winter Gardens of The Royal Hotel. The rooms formed a horse shoe shape towards the railway and the back of the building was glass so we could see what went on in the Winter Gardens – exciting Boxing matches, for example! After about 10 years we moved the business to 5 Station Road and we lived on King Edward Road.

My father taught Pete Sleight and Ron Webb all about the Kinema projection and myself if it comes to that! Once all three of them had 'flu, which was not surprising considering the sheet metal of the projection box often produced temperatures of 90 degrees and then they would go out into the cold air. Anyway, as they were all ill, I had to do it, although I was only 13. I was helped by Tiggy (Capt. Allport) – the show must go on!

My father was an enterprising business man. He used to recharge wireless batteries and, as more and more people acquired a wireless set, he found it awkward to deliver the heavy batteries so he bought a donkey chair from Johnny Wield and made a wooden platform for the batteries and took them round the village on that. His was the first shop in the village with electricity and people came to see it. We also had the first T.V., which he constructed – using a lens from the Kinema.

During the war he was responsible for the lighting and flare path at Woodhall Spa aerodrome – it was quite important work which most of the pilots realised. He never felt Guy Gibson quite appreciated it though. He thought he was a bit "stuck up" with ordinary people.

I was in the choir of St. Peter's. Miss Lunn, Florence, played the organ and boys like myself pumped it by using a lead weight on a cord, until my father introduced an electric fan, in about 1932. There were quite a lot of us in the choir, including characters like Johnny Wield and we had a bit of fun. Once we were rebuked for talking, by the Rev.d Harvey – he was a lovely man. He said he'd bring books to keep us quiet if we felt we had to be amused in church – we talked no more. There were often quite important people in the congregation from elsewhere, as well as those, like the Hotchkins, who belonged to the village. There might be London guests of the Weigalls including Princess Marie Louise. She always looked distinguished but rather old. I saw her lay the foundation stone for what was going to be the new Spa Baths in Jubilee Park. That didn't happen but the stone is still there, on a wall of the cafe.

There was very little traffic here when I was a boy, except horses and carts, of course. I sometimes went round with Frank Goodyear on his, delivering meat. Bikes were popular but you had to take care not to trap your tyres in the railway lines on the Broadway! Sometimes we bowled hoops up the Broadway. We liked climbing trees.

Silver birches don't have branches near the ground so we used to hammer nails in to start us off! When we played on the ground where the Victoria Hotel had been we dug up some of its half buried railings and used them as spears!

I remember cold winters when people skated on the fields by Tattershall Road and sometimes on the Witham, where there could be 16 inches of ice and competitions were held, skating from Lincoln to Boston. Professionals came from all over, I believe and the hot chestnut man would be on the ice. I remember horses pulling a sort of snow plough up Station Road and clearing the pavement outside the Winter Gardens.

Golfers who came usually stayed at the Golf Hotel. There was an early mechanical apparatus for golf practice in the hallway of the hotel. There was a mat about 6 feet from a screen which had the golf course pictured on it. A ball hung on a cord and the force and direction registered when it was struck.

I left Woodhall Spa in 1936, after a happy boyhood here. There were 4 of us lads in the family and, as you can imagine, we didn't go to sleep very quickly but we were always aware of my father's footsteps approaching at 10.30, after the Kinema and then we had to be quiet!

CHAPTER XI

Neil Hotchkin Esq.

Neil Stafford Hotchkin is the great grandson of Thomas Hotchkin, who initiated and financed the spa. Thomas died in 1848 but his son, Thomas John Stafford Hotchkin continued his father's support of village concerns. He made improvements and additions to the Baths and Victoria Hotel before selling the enterprise to a syndicate of gentlemen in 1886.

The syndicate employed Bath City architect, Major Davis, who remodelled The Baths and Pump Room to make them, reportedly, "The finest in Europe," with Robey & Co. of Lincoln providing new machinery which could raise 20,000 gallons of water a day. A new wing was built on the Victoria Hotel and the first season in 1888 was deemed a brilliant success, with 7,000 baths taken and over 6,000 tickets sold for musical entertainment in the Spa grounds. Thus the future of Woodhall Spa was ensured.

The Hotchkin family was at the centre of village life, the automatic choice for committees and presidencies. The grounds of "The Lodge," as the Manor House was known in the 1880s, were used for local and charitable occasions such as the annual outing of the Gartree Branch of the Girls Friendly Society. Games and lawn tennis were played and tea was provided by Mrs. Hotchkin. Thomas John Stafford became a Justice of the Peace in 1890, a year in which, as well as already holding office in various societies, he was elected Chairman of the newly formed Woodhall Spa Conservative Association. He died the following year, aged 52.

"Yes, of course, I never knew my grandfather," says Neil Hotchkin, "and my father, Stafford Vere Hotchkin, who was born in 1876, was only 15 when his father died, so he began to play his part in village affairs at an early age. He was a member of the first Urban District Council, in 1898, at the age of 22 and its Chairman seven years later." 1905 was the year in which the new, 18 hole, golf course was opened in Woodhall Spa. It was constructed on land given by Mr. Hotchkin and is now, fittingly, named "The Hotchkin Course." At its official opening, many nationally known golfers including "Open" Champions J.H. Taylor, J. Braid and Harry Vardon who had helped with the design of the course, were very impressed and it was apparent that golf would be another attraction for visitors to the Spa.

1905 was also the year when "The Dower House" was built for Mrs. Hotchkin. Her son, Stafford, was to be married the following year and would require the Manor House.

"My mother, Dorothy Arnold, was from London. She was the daughter of an Alderman. I imagine she found life in Lincolnshire very different from that of the city, although she had been here several times, of course, staying at the Victoria and, in 1906, Woodhall Spa was high society in the summer".

A baby girl, Faith, was born in 1907 but both Mr. and Mrs. Hotchkin continued the family commitment to Woodhall Spa. Like his father before him, Stafford became Chairman of the Conservative Association. He was President of the Cricket Club, the new Hockey Club, the newly formed Annual Show, to which Mrs. Hotchkin donated a silver rose bowl and, a keen cyclist, he was first President of Woodhall Spa Cycling Club, in May 1914. Mr. and Mrs. Hotchkin supported many charitable events, church bazaars and so on and, in 1914, Mrs. Hotchkin laid the foundation stone of the Home for Gentlewomen. Stafford also became a J.P., a member of the Horncastle District Council and the Horncastle Board of Guardians.

It was on 4th February 1914, that the Horncastle News reported "the residents of Woodhall Spa are highly delighted at the birth of a son, Neil Stafford Hotchkin." The report stated that Mr. and Mrs. Hotchkin and Faith were "extremely popular" and to mark the event, the

Colonel Stafford Vere Hotchkin,
M.C.

Miss Jane Newman and Mr. Neil
Hotchkin, then the captain of the
Eton cricket eleven, at a South Wold
Hunt ball at Petwood.
Cottage Museum Collection.

Captain Neil Hotchkin with some of the original
senior NCOs of 'B' troop. Standing: 'Titch'
Tindall, 'Chota' Ellis, Bill Bailey. Seated: 'Duke'
Dawson, 'Yank' Wells, Captain Hotchkin, Sid
Beech. All came from Lincoln with the exception
of Neil Hotchkin who was from Woodhall Spa and
'Chota' Ellis, who was a regular.

Opening the innings. Major Neil
Hotchkin (right) strides to the
wicket with Reg Simpson
(Nottinghamshire and, later,
England) to open the innings for the
Combined Services in India.
*From "All the King's Enemies"
by Jack Bartlett and John Benson.*

bells of St. Peter's Church rang for nearly an hour and the Union Jack was flown all day, outside the Conservative Club.

"Yes, my mother used to say "the bells <u>tolled</u> when you were born!" The Conservative Club was on the Broadway then, before the present building was built.

At the next U.D.C. meeting Mr. Hotchkin was congratulated on his son's birth. He replied that he "hoped the boy would grow up to do his duty to Woodhall Spa and Lincolnshire in the way he ought."

"I think my earliest memory is of my father coming home from the war – the First World War. He had been in Mesopotamia and was awarded the M.C. I was about 4 and I remember walking – marching, I suppose – in front of him up Manor Drive to the Manor House, waving a small Union Jack.

My next vivid memory is of the Victoria Hotel burning down, in April 1920, when I was just 6. It was Easter Sunday and there were quite a lot of people in the village. The fire started in the middle of the night. There was noise and commotion and strange light in my bedroom – the Manor House isn't far from where the Victoria stood. It was between Spa Road and the Baths. From my bedroom window I saw huge flames shooting high into the sky. I couldn't see right down to the ground as there were trees between us but the billowing flames above the dark branches made a lasting impression upon me." The hotel had just been redecorated and had a turnover of £25,000 a year when fire destroyed it, on 4th April 1920. Reputedly an electrical fault in the boiler room was the cause and fire spread to a linen room above and despite the efforts of the Woodhall and Horncastle Fire Brigades, this 150 bedroomed hotel, with suites of private apartments and imposing public rooms, burned to the ground.

"It was a catastrophe for Woodhall Spa. Wealthy and important visitors came here to the Baths, to stay at the Victoria and to say that they had stayed there. People felt that its destruction was the main cause of the village not doing so well in the early Twenties.

My father was elected Conservative Unionist M.P. for the Horncastle Division in 1920, that was when Sir Archibald Weigall, who'd held the post, was appointed Governor of South Australia. The Baths were losing money after the war and the burning down of the Victoria, so after Sir Archibald had returned in 1922, he and my father went to see the Minister of Health in London and gained permission for the Baths to be taken over by the U.D.C. Some people were against the idea because of fears as to how much it would add to the rates but already businesses were losing money and my father insisted that "the Baths must be kept open for Woodhall Spa to survive." It is interesting that the Baths never regained their former popularity, while Mr. Hotchkin's Golf Course became a great draw. After it was chosen as the venue for the English Ladies Close Championship in 1926, its first national event, increasing numbers of golfers came to Woodhall Spa. The Golf Course took over as the Baths declined.

"By this time I was away from the village for much of the year. I went to school at Sunningdale when I was 8 and then on to Eton. When I was at home in the holidays what I really wanted to do was play football and cricket – I was captain of both sports at Eton.

My sister and I had a sensible upbringing. Faith was 7 years older but we got on very well. We were always told that, while we might live in a bigger house than some children, we were just the same as everybody else. My parents were often busy with other people and my father seemed constantly to be going to meetings. There were often visitors to the house and then, of course, we were expected to behave ourselves and be polite. My mother gave afternoon teas for friends and in connection with various good works in the area and people often called to discuss things with my father. Then there were golfing and shooting parties at the house, so as children, we saw many people.

Woodhall Spa Golf Links, 5th Tee, with the Tower on the Moor to the right.
Very early days. The postmark on the card from which this is taken, is May 1905.
The new course had opened in April.

The Golf Links, Woodhall Spa. 1907.

There was sometimes a party to which Faith and I would be invited. I suppose there was a sort of social set and we were taken in cars to the Jessops at Harrington Hall, or the Rawnsleys at Well Vale, or to Petwood here. Priscilla Weigall was just 2 months younger than I was. We played party games and charades, I think and there would be some dancing. I seem to remember parties ending with "Roger de Coverley." I don't recall much about these occasions – Faith and I didn't really enjoy that sort of artificial life. Nor did Priscilla, I think. She preferred to be out of doors but her mother always wanted her to show social graces.

We did enjoy going to the Kinema! We used to sit in the front row – the first rows were deck chairs then. Sometimes, when I had been particularly engrossed I would emerge with a stripe down one cheek from the wood on the side of the deck chair! That was in the time of Captain Allport. He knew most of his customers so it was quite a social occasion.

After Eton, I read Modern Languages at Cambridge and, once again, I played football and cricket. I was fortunate to gain a Blue for cricket and may have done for football but for my predilection for horse racing at Newmarket which interfered with the Varsity team!

I played football for Woodhall and for Horncastle Town. One particular memory is of Woodhall Spa versus Horncastle, when I was playing for the Spa. We won 3-0 and I scored all three goals. I was Centre Forward so it was my job to score but it was very gratifying. The football ground here was next to the Golf Hotel, where there are bungalows now and the cricket ground was opposite the Dower Hotel, towards the Baths. I used to travel from Cambridge to play for Horncastle and then return after the match. Later I was President of the Woodhall Spa Cricket and Football Clubs for many years and still hold that position in the Football Club.

After Cambridge I was still away from Woodhall Spa, working at the Stock Exchange in London. I was in the Territorial Army 1937 and I did my early drills in London. The atmosphere was tense in the weeks before war was declared in the summer of '39. The declaration actually came on Sunday 3rd September but the Stock Exchange closed early on the preceding Friday. I drove home and next day I played golf with Claude Caswell. When I arrived home, after the round, my call up papers had been delivered. I had to report to Lincoln Barracks. I think everybody recognised that war was inevitable but the timing was sickening for me – I had just been asked if I could make myself available for the M.C.C. tour of India.

Neil's war-time experiences with the Lincolnshire Gunners in France, Egypt, India and Burma are vividly recorded in the book, "All the King's Enemies," by Jack Bartlett and John Benson. Captain Hotchkin gave a party for his men, "with plenty of beer," on a Saturday evening in Egypt and in India organised a Sports Day, described as "The happiest occasion in the history of the regiment!" These were the light-hearted moments. In 1944, Major Hotchkin commanded 88 Column-Chindits who were to fight behind Japanese lines in Burma. The hardships recorded defy description, ranging through intense heat, deluges of monsoon rain, sodden blankets, precipitous tracks on blistered feet, dense jungle, constant listening and watching for approaching enemy, total reliance on air supplies and the kindness of the Naga people, leeches, dysentery and malaria, leading to total exhaustion. The calm, ease and comfort of life in Woodhall Spa must have seemed but a dream.

"After the war I hoped to continue where I left off and play cricket for Middlesex, probably captaining the side the following year. Unfortunately that was not to be – several men from the firm had been killed in the war and I couldn't be spared."

N.B. Reputedly, several eminent cricketers expected Neil to be capped for England.

"I worked in London for 50 years, from the mid 30s to the mid 80s, usually coming home on Friday evening and leaving early on Monday morning. I remember the early days when I drove a Singer 9 car and I would leave Woodhall Spa at 5.50am and reach the Stock Exchange at 9.30.

I took more interest in golf and the Golf Club after the war. My father was becoming older and after he died the club would be my responsibility. His death in 1953, was a sadness to many people. It was just 6 months before Sallie and I were married, in February 1954. We had our house built for us, on Horncastle Road. There was a bit of interest and curiosity about it in the village, as there always is about new properties. Well, I suppose local people were used to Hotchkins in the Manor or Dower and when our garages went up first, they were mistaken by someone for the property and a rumour went round that young Mr. Hotchkin was building only a very small bungalow!

I hope I have served Woodhall Spa. Times have changed and I spent years living away. Following family tradition I was Chairman of the Conservative Association here for many years but, eventually, had to relinquish that because I was so rarely able to attend meetings. Golfing commitments have taken and still take much time, here in Woodhall, elsewhere in England and in Europe. For all my travels Sallie has supported me to the hilt in arranging them and giving me the often very necessary encouragement. I could not have succeeded without her. It is a great joy to us that the Golf Club is flourishing and so many people are able to enjoy playing the Hotchkin and now, also the Bracken Course."

Home of the English Golf Union, Woodhall Spa Golf Club is nationally and internationally known, the Hotchkin Course being rated in the top fifty in the world. Mr. Hotchkin himself is President of Woodhall Spa Golf Club and has been Patron of the Lincolnshire Union of Golf Clubs since 1984. A member of English Golf Union committees since 1954, he was elected President of the Union in 1972. He served on European Golf Association Committees from 1977 to 1993 and was President of the Association from 1989-90.

For over a century and a half, visitors have travelled to this place to enjoy activities instigated by the Hotchkin family. It has been a beneficial and happy association for Woodhall Spa.

Neil and Sallie Hotchkin in June 1998.

AS THE CENTURY ENDED

Golfers on the 17th green.

The Hotchkin Course, 18th hole.

Woodhall Spa

The Centre of Golfing Excellence

National Golf Centre, Woodhall Spa.

About the Author

Marjorie Sargeant came to live in Woodhall Spa, with her late husband and three sons, in 1971. She taught at St. Andrew's School for several years and hopes that she helped children to be lovers of wisdom beyond the necessary discipline of examinations. She remembers her grandmother telling her tales of her Victorian childhood and regrets having listened to them somewhat cursorily as she was anxious to go out to play. Perhaps this compilation is a compensation.

Although not a golfer, or, as she says, perhaps <u>because</u> she is not a golfer, Marjorie wrote a history of the club here, "A Century of Golf at Woodhall Spa", which was well received.

Marjorie enjoys travel and writing her journals upon returning. She has a bolt hole in Switzerland where she lifts her eyes to the mountains, walks and writes poetry.